AGING AND BEYOND

A Travel Guide for the Final Journey

GEOFFREY BUCKLEY

Cover Design by Brad Brizendine
Front Cover Image by Geoffrey Buckley

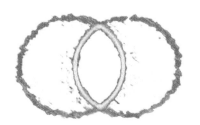

MANDORLA BOOKS
WWW.MANDORLABOOKS.COM

"After all, to the well-organized mind,
death is but the next great adventure."

~J. K. Rowling,
from *Harry Potter and the Sorcerer's Stone*

TABLE OF CONTENTS

FOREWORD

When I finished reading Dr. Geoffrey Buckley's elegant exploration, *Aging and Beyond: A Travel Guide for the Final Journey*, I felt at peace with my own aging and with what follows. As a former pastor until 1985 and a marriage and family therapist since then, Buckley is in a unique place with multiple perspectives to explore not only his own final days but all of ours. What I have liked in his earlier study, *The Practically Divine Marriage*, I am even more deeply appreciative of in this one: his courage, his kindness, his courtesy, and his contemplative, conversational tone on topics many would rather sidestep than plunge into courageously.

So, a gentle but firm encouragement, a deft image or phrase or insight are some of this book's resilient strengths. So too are the many forms of support he turns to throughout: music, classics of literature like Herman Melville's *Moby-Dick*, characters like Job from the Bible, his own paintings, his marriage and family, and his sacred space of the therapy room as well as the holiness of the church chapel.

Another throughline that holds his study together is the nature of stories themselves – one of the most efficacious ways to build community between two people or hundreds, all working to support and share their stories with others. At this juncture of writing the Foreword, I am 78 years old, a few years older than Buckley. Most often, I found my head bobbing in agreement with his conclusions and the confluences of disciplines he often wove together to arrive there.

Yet, he does not shy away from the shadow demons that haunt all of us, perhaps more saliently in eldering: resentments, remorse, loneliness, isolation, feelings of despair, and sensations of a life not worth continuing, as well as the aching grief over the loss of a life partner. And yet, I found in these discussions a deep sense of hope, of vitality, and an aging but nonetheless creative attitude towards life.

Thus, as many of us enter the last journey's path, we find in his writing both room and resolve to be kind, to help others, and to bring happiness to those whose supply is short or depleted. Yes, the final journey can also unfurl occasions for joy in serving others. One should never stop being kind, for in it we are reborn into another aspect of what makes life a meaningful journey. Geoffrey Buckley's book is a profound guide.

Dennis Patrick Slattery, Ph.D. is Distinguished Professor Emeritus in Mythological Studies at Pacifica Graduate Institute. He is the author, most recently, of *The Way of Myth: Stories' Subtle Wisdom*; *The Fictions in Our Convictions: Essays in the Cultural Imagination*; and *A Pilgrimage Beyond Belief: Spiritual Journeys through Christian and Buddhist Monasteries of the American West*.

INTRODUCTION

Autumn is really the best of the seasons; and I'm not sure that old age isn't the best part of life.

~C.S. Lewis

I painted the front cover of this book as a project for one of my psychology classes. The idea was to present a kind of Rorschach where one could project emotions onto the lone sailor in a small sailboat at sea. Looking at the high waves and dark sky on the left, some students imagined that the sailor was in trouble. Others saw the sun coming through the clouds and the light ahead. That's life. Even when we are blessed by our connections to others, we still face our future in the small craft of our life, weathering storms and high waves, and finding the courage and faith to sail forward.

At 73 years old, I'm on my final journey. I don't spend much time thinking about how the journey will end, but maybe I should; the last part of that journey will be here before I know it and I'd like to be better prepared. If you're a baby boomer and you're relatively healthy and fortunate, you may have from 10 to 20 years or more left. Your first 20 were pretty momentous, and there's no reason why your final 20 can't be meaningful and hopefully enjoyable. I'm in the same boat, trying to enjoy life while I'm here, and thinking about how to prepare to leave the planet. You're reading this book because this final journey and dying doesn't terrify you – or if it does, you're still willing to look both in the eye. That's good, because being terrified doesn't help much. And, like me, you're wondering how best to prepare for that day. I have some suggestions. My suggestions will come from seeing an average of 35-40 clients a week as a psychotherapist for the past 40 years. I was a pastor for eight years before that and a naval officer before that. I also hold a Ph.D. in clinical psychology. I mention all this to say that I've learned some things about human nature.

Of course you don't want to die – but that's beside the point, isn't it? It's likely that you're already beginning to think about the next few years – what you can look forward to, what you need to take care of, and how to prepare. Clearly, the first step is to accept the fact that, as Jack Nicholson quipped in the movie *The Evening Star*, "There's not that many more shopping days til' Christmas." You won't prepare for a journey unless you're planning to take it, and our eventual death is our next big journey. Most of the world's population agree with me about death being a journey, and apparently always have. That doesn't make it a scientific fact, but it does make it interesting. I'm not going to try to convince you about what that journey will look like. How could I? It's your journey. But I do think that it makes sense to prepare for it. This won't be a book about psychology, theology, or biology. Rather, think of it as a travel guide.

It may be that what inspired me to write this book has to do with how much I enjoy denial – that lovely cushion against unpleasant realities. There are aspects of the psychological defense of denial that are truly beneficial. As youngsters in the 50s during the Cold War, denial sheltered us from the paralytic dread of imminent nuclear annihilation. We simply didn't think about it. Yes, air raid sirens were periodically tested, and we had drop drills at school. I recall that a student in class would be designated to close all the classroom blinds against the explosion of shattered glass from an atomic blast. But few of us youngsters really took the whole thing very seriously, thanks to denial.

People without this very helpful psychological defense of denial are chronically anxious. They are accustomed to imagining the worst. It may be hard for them to drive on the freeway or get into an airplane. In severe cases, they are phobic about germs or even leaving the house – certain that something bad will happen. Denial helps most of us be aware of things that could possibly go wrong, but probably won't. But too much denial isn't good, either. It prevents us from being more realistic and making wise decisions about our health and our future. Too much denial can lead to making really bad decisions.

It's easy for most of us to be in denial about the inevitability of death. In fact, Ernest Becker wrote a book about it called *The Denial of Death,* for which he won a Pulitzer Prize in 1976. I'll discuss that book in a later chapter. The point is that it's deadly to be in denial of death. We older folks need to think about and prepare for some things. We are much better off facing the facts about aging, our health, and the essential truth about the reality that our life will end.

I'll review and recommend some resources I think will be useful for your journey. Think of these as signs posted in special areas of interest along the way. I hope you are interested and do some reading – the idea of our final journey is less disturbing when you've given it some thought and made some preparations.

Chapter 1 of this travel guide is about preparing for your journey – your map, your compass, a guide for your journey, and what you'd like to take with you. I also discuss what to leave behind and the best way to get to where you're going. Chapter 2 will focus on your journey so far and some things to do along the way. The title of Chapter 3, "So What's Your Story?" is an overview of the brain's ability to construct stories about experiences, and the choices we have within those stories. Chapter 4, "Help Along the Way," explores something we need from time to time. Chapter 5 is a review of an important 2021 book titled *Being Mortal* by the physician Atul Gawande. Chapter 6 is titled "Goodness, Beauty, and Gratitude." Chapter 7 is about the importance of creativity and community. Chapter 8 is titled "Why Bother?" and explores depression, isolation, and the feelings of helplessness. Chapter 9 describes the difference between having a good death or a bad one. Chapter 10 is a discussion of memorial services. Chapter 11 discusses the value of traveling with dignity. Chapter 12 is titled "Guilt, Shame, and Sorrow." Chapter 13 is titled "When the Journey is Hard: Job, Suffering, and Rocks in the Road." Chapter 14 is about the challenge of retirement. Chapter 15 reviews the book *After,* which is about near-death experiences by Dr. Bruce Greyson. Chapter 16 is titled "Memories." Chapter 17, "From Strength to Strength," contains quotes from a book with the same title by Arthur Brooks.

You'll find that the chapters reiterate and repeat ideas from earlier chapters, and that's purposeful – it seems to me that the best ideas are worthy of returning to again and again in different contexts. Or maybe this is caused by my ADD or my tendency to get a bit preachy and repetitive. You will notice, for example, that some parts of the book read like classroom instructions. Some parts seem like a sermon, and some parts read like the advice of a therapist. I seem to change hats a lot. Nonetheless, I'm sure you'll find value in these pages, even as we revisit certain ideas again and again, just as travelers know the value of revisiting different cities or states or countries for the joy and satisfaction of knowing them more deeply.

I have a friend who is grieving the loss of her husband of sixty-five years. I can't begin to imagine what that is like for her. She told me recently that she feels like a part of her is missing.

Of course she does. These are two people who have loved each other intensely for most of their lives. His journey here has ended, but hers continues. What could you say to her that would be at all comforting? There is very little I can think to say that doesn't sound trite. Fortunately, she found the right words herself. She told me, "When the pain of losing him becomes too intense, I'm reminded of how grateful I am to have had all of those years of happiness." I sincerely hope that her final journey is not characterized by loss alone, but also by the feeling of having been blessed with knowing love.

In the following pages, I invite you to consider your own journey. Where has your journey taken you so far? What challenges are you facing? Can you see the road ahead? How will you prepare for the next part of your journey? I hope these chapters will encourage you to give some thought to your life so far and to your life ahead.

~Geoff Buckley, April 2023

CHAPTER 1

———— • ————

PREPARATION FOR THE JOURNEY

Who is old and doesn't believe it, will trip into his grave without seeing it.

~Chris Hedges

Your Map

It's good to have a map. Remember the days when we used maps to tell us how to get somewhere? Your smart phone will give you directions, but you have to tell it where you want to go. Your map is a plan. Where would you like to end up? You have some – but not many – options. For example, when you get to the end of your journey, would you like to be buried, cremated, or leave the decision to someone else? Would you like to be scattered at sea or to the four winds? If you'd like to be buried, do you have a favorite place in mind? It isn't too early to think about that. My plan is to be buried at the cemetery in the city where I've spent the last forty-five years. My parents are buried in a cemetery thirty-six miles away, but I don't think they'd mind if I don't join them nearby. They bought their plot many years ago before the real estate boom made it too expensive for me.

I remember my grandmother taking me up to see where her husband, my grandfather, was buried at Mt. Prospect Cemetery in Franklinville, New York. As a young boy, I used to walk up to Cemetery Hill on my visits to my grandparents. It's such a peaceful and beautiful place. I would sit on a bench under the towering elms and maples and "listen" to the many stories that I imagined were all around me. I wondered, were they good stories, filled with love and laughs or tragic stories of heartache and loss? We are all living in a story. Have you thought much about your own story? We love stories about people who face difficulties and overcome challenges, learn valuable lessons and make a difference. Is that your story?

Before Grandma died, she and I walked up to "visit" Grandpa. "See," Grandma said, "They've got a spot for me right there next to Ed." Then she looked up at me with her blue eyes and impish grin and said, "Cours' you and I both know that I won't really be there." She must have known that her prospects were good. I think her humor and faith-filled acceptance of her own and her husband's life's end have truly been a lifelong gift to me.

What's the point of having a plan, you may ask? My answer is that I would prefer to do the dirty (sorry) work rather than have it fall to a family member. I'm guessing that when I die, I will be missed. My family will have mixed feelings. Being Christians, they'll know that I'm okay, but being human, they'll feel sad for their loss – time will tell. In any case, I followed the example of my parents and bought my spot early before I was priced out of the market. I'd like to make sure I haven't left a lot of bother for my family when I'm gone. Below are some other considerations as you plan for your next journey.

An Advanced Directive

According to the American Cancer Society:

> An advance directive is a legal document that explains how you want medical decisions about you to be made if you cannot make the decisions yourself. An advance directive lets your health care team and loved ones know what kind of health care you want, or who you want to make decisions for you when you can't. An advance directive can help you think ahead of time about what kind of care you want. It may help guide your loved

ones and health care team in making clear decisions about your health care when you can't do it yourself.

My doctor forgets that I do have an advanced directive on file and keeps asking me about it. Does she know something I don't!? It's completely understandable that folks don't want to think about or talk about dying. "Mom, that's years away! We don't need to talk about that now," is a common response when our moms bring up the topic. Nonetheless, it's good for the family to know where your important papers are stored, including your will, insurance information, funeral arrangements, advanced directive, and whatever else they need to know.

Throughout this travel guide, I'll suggest additional books to read or review - points of interest if you like. On top of the list is *Being Mortal* by Atul Gawande. Gawande writes at great length about the value of having a plan. This is especially important as you enter the last phase of your life's journey. At least read the chapter on "Letting Go." That chapter contains vital information about the value of discussing your wishes for your final days. It may seem counterintuitive, but, according to Gawande, talking about those last days, instead of plunging you into depression and freaking out your family members, actually improves your emotional and mental health and possibly gives you additional time, and quality time with your loved ones. Instead of being unprepared and taken by surprise, discussing your wishes with your family and physicians can be a valuable way to encourage acceptance and peace. Of course, this requires not being in denial and somehow counting on God or your doctor to provide a miracle.

Miracles do happen. We hear about them all the time. The problem, of course, is that if you could count on it, it wouldn't be a miracle. This is a challenge for religious people. Do we pray for a miracle or simply leave the situation in God's hands, or both? Is it a lack of faith not to believe that God can heal someone? Do we follow the advice of the poet Dylan Thomas to "rage against the dying of the light?" or accept the advice of Solomon in the Bible that for everything there is a season, a time to be born and a time to die? Or maybe we should simply try to balance loving life while accepting death. That's the decision I've made. I don't fear death - it's the dying part I wish I could avoid.

Like many of us, I don't like to think about being fragile, needing a walker, or lying in a hospital bed. I'll try to enjoy my life as much as possible while still here.

A Guide for Your Journey

Whether you're aware of it or not, you have an inner guide - a quiet voice in your head and heart that may be able to sense the best direction for you to take. You may not have consulted this "inner" guide for a while. Maybe you never have. Now's the time. Better late than…. Some people have regular conversations with this inner guide. The guide may be your logic, your intuition, your sense of God's voice, or maybe all three. This inner guide may encourage you to consult with others. In my mind, family members and good friends should be consulted. If you're over 75, why put it off any longer? They may be interested in your plans. They may suggest some things you haven't thought about or have avoided thinking about. Consulting others is useful, but how to make the journey is ultimately your decision. Starting out in life, we don't seem to choose what interests us, what appeals to us, and what doesn't. We either will or won't select paths based on what appeals to us. Following your inner guide can sometimes be as easy as "I like this - I don't like that."

Have you read or heard about an allegorical journey Dante Alighieri wrote about in the early 1300s? He wrote it as a trilogy titled *Inferno, Purgatorio*, and *Paradiso*. It's a story about a journey down to hell. He wrote about finding himself in a dark wood where every path out of the woods was blocked by a ferocious beast. He prayed that God would help him. God sent him a guide in the person of a favorite ancient Roman poet, Virgil, and later, his guide was Beatrice, a beautiful woman he respected and loved from afar. Is Dante telling us that we find a way out of our dark woods with the help of beauty and love? What's that about? And what if we haven't known or listened to that inner guide? We'll explore those questions later. Back to Dante, in his allegorical poem, he successfully made it through his journey, but had to visit some very dark places en route. Like all good art, his poem has a lot to teach us about the important lessons we have to learn on our own life's journey. If you're interested, read *Dark Wood to White Rose: Journey and Transformation in Dante's Divine Comedy* written by Helen Luke in 1993.

What to Take With You

On this final journey, you won't need much. Take your memories, especially the memories of the things you are grateful for. Take the feelings of having been loved – if you've been fortunate. And, if you've been fortunate, you can take the knowledge that you've made a contribution to life. I use the term "fortunate" because so many people haven't been. Perhaps they weren't wanted as children. Perhaps they grew up disadvantaged or in poverty. Many people simply do the best they can to survive. However unfortunate someone may be, it's still possible to make a contribution of some kind. I like Ernest Becker's conclusion in *The Denial of Death*. He writes: "The most that anyone can seem to do is to fashion something – an object or ourselves – and drop it into the confusion, make an offering of it so to speak, to the life force." I think Becker's observation is right. Most of us probably won't change the world, but we can make a difference. We can create something of value, maybe even our own life, and offer it to the world.

I believe that kindness may be our best contribution. You might be surprised how a simple smile might save someone's life. If you watch the YouTube video "I Jumped Off the Golden Gate Bridge," you'll out that the jumper might not have jumped if he had felt like someone cared. A couple of visiting tourists approached him on the bridge. I think he was secretly hoping that they were interested in him and would be friendly. When they simply wanted him to take their picture, it convinced him that no one truly cared – that he was alone. He said on the video that as soon as he leapt from the bridge he knew it was a mistake and regretted it, but it was too late. Luckily, he was one of the very few who survived the fall and the icy water of the bay. A Coast Guard vessel just happened to be close by to pull him out.

I try to smile and be kind. It isn't hard. I've taken small Christmas gifts to the tellers at my bank, helped guys load lumber at Home Depot, picked up litter that fell out of my neighbors' trash can. This didn't take much effort. I'm simply illustrating how easy it is to be kind. Even I can do that, and I bet you can think of kindnesses you've shown to others. I also imagine that you can think of many other contributions you've made. If you can't, there's still time.

No one liked Ebenezer Scrooge. He probably didn't like himself. Charles Dickens, the author of *A Christmas Carol*, pre-dated Freud and other psychologists when he sent four ghosts to visit Scrooge on Christmas Eve. Three of the ghosts represented three types of classic psychotherapy: Marley, the first ghost, warned Scrooge that he needed to learn some important lessons. The Ghost of Christmas Past took Ebenezer back to his childhood to revisit the wounds of his mother having died birthing him, and his father resenting and abandoning him. No wonder Scrooge was bitter. The Ghost of Christmas Present took him through the streets of London and to the meager but joyful Christmas celebration of a close family at the Cratchit household. The ghost wasn't singing "Don't worry, be happy!" but he might as well have been. It doesn't take much, according to the Ghost, to spread joy to others. But it was the Ghost of Things Yet to Come that finally got to Ebenezer and convinced him to make a difference while there was still time. Neither psychodynamic therapy (reviewing your childhood) nor cognitive-behavioral therapy (don't think that way, think this way) did the trick. So, Dickens sent Scrooge an existential intervention (thinking about what is ultimately valuable). Looking into his future grave, Scrooge realized that his life had meant nothing to anyone and promised to make some changes.

Scrooge woke up Christmas morning, a changed man. He became kind. He was kind to his nephew, Fred, to his employee, Bob Cratchit, to Tiny Tim, and to the poor and needy of London. And in making a contribution, he was kind to himself. He could take something with him. Read the *Power of Kindness* by Piero Ferrucci for some helpful tips. There may be no greater reward in life than to know that you were kind to others. Hopefully, in your memorial service, they will say that they remember how kind you were. What else can you take besides your memories, your gratitude for the gift of life, the feeling of being loved, and the knowledge that you had been kind – your simple, yet significant contributions? That may be enough.

What to Leave Behind

This one's easy. What do you leave behind? Everything. Well, not quite everything. Leave behind the work you've done to love your family and friends, the memories and happiness you have given to others, the kind and generous things that have added up over a lifetime. Your life has been valuable. Leave behind a smile, knowing that your life was an adventure.

If you can't smile, and many can't, leave behind your bitterness. Life isn't fair. It never has been. It never will be. People may have hurt you, betrayed you, lied to others about you. You may not want to, but you know that it would be good to forgive them and let it go. Forgiveness is hard. Keep in mind that when you forgive someone you're not saying, "It's okay, it's in the past." No! It likely wasn't okay and the hurt and anger may still be with you. The best way to think about forgiveness is *to transfer judgment to God*. He is the best judge. Also, it's important to forgive yourself. Try to leave behind your regrets. I would love to think that our pilgrimage on earth is a time for learning. I would like to think we'll wake up on the other side, rub our eyes and say, "Wow, that was interesting!" I hope that we have learned what we needed to learn. And the most important lesson of this life is the value of love. Scripture promises us that our future holds no tears and no regrets, only love.

You may have heard the saying that there's no U-Haul trailer behind a hearse. Whatever you need to take care of while you're still here, you probably need to do it soon. You don't want to leave with a lot of baggage, with unfinished work. Too many people do too little to prepare for their last journey. That's understandable. There are many more pleasant things to do and think about. But you already know how fast time flies. So, if you haven't done so already, it's time to think about creating a will or living trust, deciding on an advanced directive, plans for your memorial service, and what to do about your remains. Remains, that's an interesting word, isn't it? It suggests that there is more of you than what's left behind. What do you think about the idea of having a soul that lives on? What could that mean?

What's a Soul? Is It Important to Know?

"Soul" is the English translation for the Greek word "psyche." The ancient Greeks believed that the soul was the divine aspect of a human being that continued on after the death of the body. It seems that human beings have always believed in some sort of afterlife. That's what Professor Reza Aslan concludes from his exhaustive research into human history: "Human beings intuitively knew that they are embodied souls. It is a belief so primal and innate, so deep-rooted and widespread, that it must be considered nothing less than the hallmark of the human experience."

The ancient Greeks tended to give names to their beliefs and personify them in mortals and gods. For example, the concept of an eternal soul was named Psyche. In the Greek mind, Psyche was a mortal woman who fell in love with the god Eros. The Greeks understood that there are certain dynamics of human experience that don't seem to change - there are archetypal themes that play out again and again. For example, if we try to emulate the god Apollo by living a one-dimensional life of too much work and responsibility, we will likely be visited by the god *Dionysus*. Dionysus, the god of intoxication, ecstasy, and madness comes calling when we don't pay attention to living a balanced life. It's interesting that the introduction to the hit television series *Mad Men* shows a guy entering his office, setting his briefcase down, and shortly finds himself in a free fall out of the office window. The lead character, Don Draper, shows us what happens when you dance with Dionysus.

Back to Psyche, your soul. On the next page is John William Waterhouse's painting titled "Psyche Opening the Door of Cupid's Garden." Cupid is the Roman name for the Greek god Eros.

When you hear or see the word "erotic" you'll likely think of sex. That's okay, we all do. That's part of what the word means. But Eros symbolizes more than sex. The word "eros" also refers to "life force." The most powerful life force for human beings is love. Notice in the painting, Psyche is always looking for Eros, telling us that the human soul is constantly searching for love. Of course it does, or there would be no Hallmark Channel or 60s songs. People love love. Always have. Is that the reason that it's so hard to give up life?

In his 2020 book, *Together*, the current U.S. Surgeon General Dr. Vivek Murthy writes that humans are hardwired for connection. Psyche is always searching for Eros. The soul knows that it is supposed to experience love and connection. Which is why loneliness and lovelessness is so devastating. So, while you're still here, consider that you may have some deep knowledge of what has always been true: love, connection, and, perhaps, even an eternal soul.

As far as I can tell, research into the world's religions suggests that a commonality in the world's faiths is the value of love – loving God and loving others. The Greeks had three principal words for love: Eros (connection), Philia (love of kindred), and Agape (unconditional love). I like how M. Scott Peck describes agape in his book *The Road Less Traveled*. He defines love as "the will to extend one's self for the purpose of nurturing one's own or another's spiritual growth." I think by using the term "spiritual growth," Peck is describing someone's ultimate well-being. The psychologist Rollo May wrote a book titled *Love and Will*. He joins Peck in locating the heart of love in the willingness to extend yourself to others. Have you experienced love? Have you loved? If so, savor the experience and thank God for it. If you haven't, there's still time. Think about where you can go and what you can do to connect with people. Since there's still time, find people to be kind to and, when possible, to love. It's important.

Your Compass

We've talked in this chapter about what to take with you on your journey, what to leave behind, and the importance of love and the soul. In addition, when preparing for your journey, it's good to have a compass – some idea of where you're going and how to get there. Below is a ship's compass. Once, this was essential for keeping the ship on course. Less so today – modern instrumentation and GPS have eclipsed the need to steer the ship's course solely by the compass.

Give some thought to your life, where you've been, where you're headed. It's good for your mental health. Do you have some goals yet to attain? Do you have some unfinished business to take care of? Are there people you need to talk to?

The psychologist Eric Fromm said that all human beings have five "existential" needs that are important for our existence and well-being as humans. Fromm believed we all need relationships, our connections to others. We also need a sense of our own individual identity.

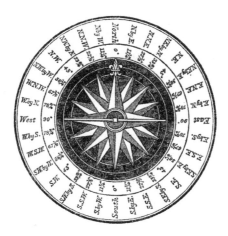

We need roots – some sort of home base, family, or location, or the values, beliefs, and traditions that support us as we age and give us a sense of stability and connection. But because it's possible to become too comfortable and stagnant or closed-minded, we also need a sense of the transcendent – something to experience or believe that elevates and transforms our perspectives. Finally, we need what Fromm referred to as "a frame of orientation," a way to think about and make sense of life. Below is a diagram of what Fromm was saying:

Do you have a frame of orientation, an overarching philosophy of life? Why is that important? The short answer is that it just may extend your life. Take a look at Richard Leiter's 2015 book, *The Power of Purpose*. You'll notice the many physical, psychological, and spiritual benefits of spending some time contemplating your life's purpose.

Basic Needs

In Boy Scouts, we were taught that any time we journeyed into the wilderness we needed to carry 10 essentials. You can probably guess what some of those are. When the psychologist Abraham Maslow wrote about essentials, he had another list in mind, a human being's "hierarchy of human needs." The bottom level of that hierarchy is our need for food, water, and shelter. It's a shame that across the globe, so many struggle to meet those basic needs. The next higher level is safety. Again, far too many people on earth have daily concerns about their safety, even in developed countries. If people have achieved safety and subsistence, they might hope for a sense of belonging and even love, the next level on the hierarchy of needs. Clearly, Maslow did not imagine that these needs would be met in a linear progression. People have been known to fall in love in a war zone and with little to eat. But the idea is that these basic human needs are necessary for well-being, and by meeting those needs, a person could progress to a state of fulfillment, or what Maslow termed "self-actualization." I define self-actualization as the confluence of doing and being – the ultimate well-being is connecting what you do with who you are.

Do laborers on a job site or workers on an assembly line feel self-actualized? Maybe not. Maybe they are satisfied with simply helping to put food on the table. There may not be a direct confluence between who they are and what they're doing at work, but it's still possible to achieve self-actualization. Maslow listed some of the characteristics of a self-actualized person. On the top of the list is self-acceptance, then acceptance of others, followed by acceptance of what life has in store. If someone doesn't consider *what* they do to be intrinsically valuable, the *way* they do it can be. In another chapter, I'll discuss ways to acquire a sense of self-acceptance and acceptance of others and what life has in store – a sense of self-actualization. For now, it is enough to know that an important stop on your journey is to consider who you are and why you're here.

Why Are You Here?

Have you asked yourself that question, why am I here? It's helpful to have an answer. Why? This chapter is about preparing for the journey ahead. It's easier to face the end of your life when you have had a meaningful life. You often hear older people say, "I've had a good life." Why do they say that? I think it's because it's important to feel like you've made the most of the gift of life.

In the movie *Saving Private Ryan*, an older Ryan, looking down at the grave of his rescuer, Captain Miller, says to his wife, "Tell me I've lived a good life - tell me I'm a good man." Why ask that question? Because he knew that he owed his own life to the sacrifices of the men who rescued him. It seems important to people to believe that their time on earth was valuable in some way, that they made a difference, that their life wasn't wasted.

Our dog Martha (she preferred to be called Maggie) and I used to go on walks in the hills above our house. Maggie would spot a rabbit and off she went. She never managed to catch one, but she would return shortly wagging her tail, having enjoyed the chase. The rabbit, lighting out in instinctive panic, would soon realize that the danger had passed and would go back to grazing, not especially worried that Maggie was becoming clever and, "one of these days," might be able to catch him.

Rabbits don't think about "one of these days" - humans do. If we have the luxury to think about more than simply surviving, we think about what life is all about. And I believe that what life is about, in the final analysis, is learning about love. Why are you here? My answer? To experience love and to bring love to others. It's that simple.

How many songs can you think of that focus on love - finding it, losing it, needing it, celebrating it? How many movies have you watched where the concluding scene celebrates love? Lovers find each other, struggle through challenges, and eventually celebrate love's triumph. Why is that a great end to a movie? Because all of us know that that's what life is all about. These movies simply remind us about what we already know.

Why do you imagine I'm bringing this up in a chapter about how to prepare to die? The song "El Paso" gives us a clue. Marty Robbins recorded the song in his album *Gunfighter Ballads*. The song was a hit on both country and pop music charts, becoming No. 1 in both areas in the early 60s, and winning a Grammy Award for Best Country & Western Recording in 1961. The last line of the song is "One little kiss and Feleena, goodbye." Having escaped the consequences of a jealous murder, Feleena's suitor risks his life returning to his Mexican maiden in El Paso. The friends of the murdered cowboy discover his return; they chase him, riding fast toward the town and firing several lethal shots. The cowboy makes it to Rosa's Cantina and dies in the arms of Felenna.

Is love that powerful, that someone would knowingly risk their life for it? Or was the cowboy just being ridiculous and stupid? Evidently, the thousands of people who love that song must have imagined that love *can* be that powerful – powerful enough to risk one's life. I suppose that when people say that they've "had a good life," it's because they've experienced love. They've accepted that the many sacrifices and hardships of life are the cost of finding, offering, and holding on to love. Can you say that you have had a good life? Have you experienced love? Have you loved? If so, you are prepared. You have lived.

Love doesn't always have to be the romantic kind that we hear in songs or watch at the movies. Love can be between good friends or family members. Not long before he died, my dad said that he had married his best friend. He also said that he'd had a good life. He and Mom showed me that love doesn't always have to be romantic to be powerful. I have a friend who I talk with on the phone nearly every week. The love of her life is her little grandniece who visits her on a regular basis. My friend lives near her extended family, and her voice changes perceptibly when she talks about the fun she has with her niece. Being loved and enjoyed in this way will be among the most important and precious resources that this little girl will take with her on the rest of her own journey.

CHAPTER 2

———— • ————

YOUR JOURNEY SO FAR

Like Pilgrims to th' appointed place we tend;
The world's an inn, and death the journey's end.

~John Dryden

Thinking About Your Life

Most of us have probably spent some time thinking about our life. That may be uncomfortable for some, but it's still a good thing to do. You're still alive and likely have some time left to reflect on your life and, perhaps, make some changes. If your life has worked out pretty much the way you had hoped, it's something you can enjoy thinking about, talking about, and being grateful about. You can share your story with your family and maybe some friends, enjoy looking at photos, and reminiscing a bit about the old days. I'd like to amend the quote above: death is *this* journey's end, but who knows what the next journey will look like.

It's a good thing to think about your life as you prepare for the next phase of your journey. It's good to think about what you've accomplished, the people you've touched or helped along the way, the children you've raised or helped to raise, the legacy of how people will remember you. It's good to feel good about the life you've lived. There are many different types of memory books in which you can record some of the highlights of your life. Family members may want to read and remember some of the stories about the life you've led.

In 1950, the psychologist Erik Erikson wrote about the eight significant stages of life in his book *Childhood and Society.* Erikson titled the final stage of life "integrity vs. despair." For Erikson, the task of life at that stage is to develop an outlook about one's life, and acceptance of eventual death. "Integrity" for Erikson wasn't about honesty or good behavior, but about things holding together. In the Navy, we used the term "watertight integrity," which meant that there were no leaks. A life that is lived well holds together: it doesn't leak. A good life isn't a perfect life – that doesn't exist. It's a life well lived where we can look back with gratitude that there weren't very many leaks.

The alternative, Erikson wrote, is despair. The despair that many people feel towards the end of their lives typically centers around choices that could have been made but weren't. Bad choices, regrets, resentments, unlived potentials, and bitterness about what could or should have worked out – all these can easily lead to a sense of depression and despair. I don't know what percentage of people resolve that final stage of life successfully, the way they would have wished. I suspect not many, because life takes its toll on us. It would be surprising to get to the end of life with no significant regrets.

Erikson wrote about the stages of life in the 50s, but people are living longer in the 21st century. Gene Cohen wrote *The Mature Mind: The Positive Power of the Aging Brain* in 2016. He wrote that older adults continue to feel an inner push toward being productive, useful, and creative. He added four additional life stages for older adults. These stages are: Midlife Reevaluation (ages 50-70); Liberation (ages late 50s into the 70s); Summing Up (ages 60s-80s) and Final Stage, Encore (late 70s to the end of life). An introduction to The *Mature Mind* states that:

The Golden Years are being redefined. The fastest-growing segment of the population, those beyond the age of fifty, are no longer content to simply cope with the losses of age. Mental acuity and vitality are becoming a life-long pursuit. Now, the science of the mind is catching up with the Baby Boom generation. In this landmark book, renowned psychiatrist Gene Cohen challenges the long-held belief that our brain power inevitably declines as we age and shows that there are actually positive changes taking place in our minds. Based on the latest studies of the brain, as well as moving stories of men and women in the second half of life, *The Mature Mind* reveals for the first time how we can continue to grow and flourish. Cohen's groundbreaking theory – the first to elaborate on the psychology of later life – describes how the mind gives us "inner pushes" and creates new opportunities for positive change throughout adult life. He shows how we can jump-start that growth at any age and under any circumstances, fine-tuning as we go, actively building brain reserves and new possibilities. *The Mature Mind* offers a profoundly different and intriguing look at ourselves, challenging old assumptions, raising bold new questions, and providing exciting answers grounded in science and the realities of everyday life.

How pleasant it is, at the end of the day,
No follies to have to repent:
But reflect on the past, and be able to say,
That my time has been properly spent.

~Jane Taylor

Your Life So Far

Youth is the gift of nature but age is a work of art.

~Stanislaw Jerzy Lec

If you're reading this book, you're likely in the second half of your life. You wouldn't have been very interested in your final journey as a healthy younger person. You were focused on what was right in front of you. That's good. The first half of life is about learning how to survive. It's usually not until you reach the second half of your life, sometime in your mid to late 40s, that you begin to evaluate how you're doing with your life and you look ahead to the next part of your journey. In this chapter, we will explore what it is to be a human being and what you have accomplished on your journey so far. It's good to look back at where you've been in order to better prepare for where you're going, or what you may have left to do, or simply to give you a sense of your life's completion. Let's begin by looking at human nature.

You were born into a particular family and culture at a particular time in history. Your job was to stay alive, learn the rules and expectations of your family and culture, and prepare for your future. Nature and nurture worked together to give you a start at whom you have become. *Nature* provided you with DNA from your parents and ancestors. *Nurture* was at work in your childhood and cultural conditioning, molding you into someone who understood the context of your time on earth and equipped you, for better or worse, for existing in that context. So, how are you doing so far?

You've had to make decisions. In fact, making decisions is what makes you human. There are many ways to define a human being or to explore human nature. You can look at history, biology, psychology, and the social sciences. But the central fact of human life is that human beings make lots of decisions. A good source for grasping this vital aspect of human nature is in the beautiful language of the Bible.

The Book of Genesis collapses the history of human origin into a beautiful and even poetic shorthand. According to Scripture, God lovingly molded the first human being from dirt, breathed into the dirt, and humankind had its beginning. Breath (spirit) was breathed into dirt (biology) and the intersection of the two became "soul." According to Genesis, God spoke the worlds into existence, from the expanse of the cosmos to the tiniest micro-organisms on earth. But God did something different with human beings. God spoke *to* human beings. "And God blessed them and *said* to them...." Genesis is a good way to understand what it is to be a human being. Genesis declares that we are endowed with the *ability to respond.* In other words, we have "response-ability." We have response-ability to each other, to the earth, and to what is transcendent and sacred. Not to be responsible to our response-ability is a contradiction of our human nature – at its worst, it's the origin of all the bad we do to the planet and to each other.

As I mentioned in the last chapter, the word "soul" comes from the Greek "psyche." Psychology is the study of the soul. It is the study of the challenges of being human and the best ways to meet those challenges. We have decisions to make, many decisions. Our soul, our psychology, is the crucible in which those decisions are tested. Thinking psychologically, the human soul is the place of connection and tension between our spirit (what is possible for us and what is eternally valuable) and our biology (the necessities required in living in a finite body). It is in our psychology that we wrestle with the challenges of being a human being, the challenges of managing the tug-o-war between flesh and spirit, between possibility and necessity.

Abraham Lincoln used the phrase "the better angels of our nature." A person recovering from addiction may call it our "higher power." Both are referring to the human capacity to be response-able to "spirit," our innate capacity to know the right direction, to choose the correct path for our life. However, spirit often wrestles with biology, and our soul is the place in which that wrestling takes place – in the connection between spirit and biology. This is the essence of being human, a life-long wrestling match with decisions. You are at a stage in life where you can look back and see how those choices have worked out. This looking back may be both joyful or painful, depending on the decisions you made at the time. It makes sense to assess what you have learned so far and encourage others to make the same or different choices.

The First Half of Life

In the first half of our life, we learned about who we are and what was expected of us. We discovered the wonder and work of living in a body. We were taught the predominant language of our culture and how to use that language successfully. We were taught how to live among other people and how to survive in our culture. We discovered the diversity of directions we can choose for our life's journey.

A lot happens in the first half of our life. Psychologists think of this phase of life as a time of ego development. The term "ego" refers to our ability to relate successfully to the world around us. Our ego is tasked with learning about what is important in our culture, the tools we will need to fit in, to survive, and to compete for what we're taught are the right kinds of achievements. At the same time, we also acquire a sense of who we are as individuals – the ways in which we are unique. This can be confusing at times, especially in later adolescence, when we measure our value against the background of societal values and against what we, as individuals, value. We have to make decisions. Which of the variety of values that are presented to us are genuinely valuable? For better or worse, this is the work of soul-making.

Let's look briefly at your life so far. As I mentioned earlier, psychologist Eric Erickson believed people (in developed countries) tend to go through various stages in life. These stages are somewhat linear – but not entirely. Erikson said that a person who meets most of the developmental tasks at one age is better prepared to move on to the next developmental stage. If the greater percentage of developmental tasks haven't been accomplished successfully at one age, they may be delayed into later years. Ideally, as we go through life, we continue to work on becoming increasingly mature.

Erikson's Eight Stages of Psychosocial Development (A Closer Look)

When Erik Erikson wrote *Childhood and Society,* he addressed ego development throughout the lifespan. He wrote about eight major stages of life from childhood through old age. Each stage of development presents options for success or failure in achieving progressive developmental tasks. He termed these stages "psycho-social-crises." The term "crises" refers to focused demands on the ego to meet the developmental challenges appropriate to that age. I've listed these developmental challenges:

0-2 years old: Trust vs. Mistrust
2-3 years old: Autonomy vs. Shame and Doubt
3-5 years old: Initiative vs. Guilt
5-12 years old: Industry vs. Inferiority
12-18 years old: Identity vs. Role Confusion
18-40 years old: Intimacy vs. Isolation
40-65 years old: Generativity vs. Stagnation
65+ years old: Integrity vs. Despair

It's interesting to look back on your life to see how you did in meeting these challenges. Bear in mind that he wrote about these stages in the 50s in a Western cultural context, and things have changed since then, but the stages are still valuable to consider. Since he didn't imagine that each stage would be fully completed in a linear progression, we can look back on our lives and continue to work on improving ourselves at each developmental level.

Let's look at each stage in more detail.

Trust vs. Mistrust (0-2 years old)

Sometime before you were two years old, if you were fed when you were hungry, your diaper was changed when needed, and you were held when you needed comforting, you likely concluded that the world was a safe place to be. You trusted that your needs would be met on a regular basis. If those needs were met haphazardly, unpredictably, or inadequately, you wouldn't be able to trust anyone. In fact, trust may still be a bit challenging today. If your need for food and hygiene were not met at all, you wouldn't be alive to read this.

Autonomy vs. Shame and Doubt (2-3 years old)

Most people alive today had adequate nurturing or they wouldn't be alive. That doesn't necessarily mean that they are good at trusting people, trusting that their needs are important, or trusting that they have value. But for you, as an infant, if learning to trust people was sufficient, next you experimented with rolling over, crawling, and taking your first steps. If all of that was successful, praised, and encouraged, you would begin to develop a sense of autonomy. Autonomy is an interesting word. It has at least two meanings. "Auto" is from the Greek "self" and "nomos" is from the Greek "law." So that can mean "self-regulation" (which is what I think Erikson had in mind), or it could mean "a law onto oneself" (which is what most parents have experienced and called "the terrible twos"!). You may not be surprised to know that some people never grow out of that stage. They continue to be a law onto themselves. I'm sure we all know people like that.

My little daughter enjoyed pulling all of the pots and pans out of the lower kitchen cabinets just because she could. When she was a little older, she crayoned a green alligator on her bedroom wall. Parents are frequently challenged with the dilemma of how to guide or correct a toddler without shaming them and damaging their initiative. Too much correction and control create shame and doubt. I stood looking at her beautiful crayon creation trying to decide whether to punish her for crayoning on the wall or praise her for her artistic ability. I decided to do both, but in a different order. After announcing appreciation for her artistic ability, I reminded her that we have paper for crayoning. Together we bought some crayon remover, and her "punishment" (I prefer the word "consequence") was to help me scrub the crayon off the wall.

Initiative vs. Guilt (3-5 years old) and
Industry vs. Inferiority (5-12 years old)

Kids are naturally industrious – unless they are made to feel inferior or guilty. Their initiative includes exercising their wonderful imaginations, playing elaborately with toys and dolls, making things, building things, and developing fun games and pastimes. Hopefully these examples trigger some good memories for you. If so, you were permitted, perhaps encouraged, to develop your initiative – you learned to feel good about what you could do. If your imagination and creativity were stifled, you may have felt some feelings of inferiority and guilt. How about now? Can you try new things, take up new hobbies or sports? Do you feel adequately creative in some area? It's very possible to unlearn the habit of doubting yourself and developing more confidence in trying new things. I'll discuss how in another chapter.

Identity vs. Role Confusion (12-18 years old)

What were you like as a teenager? Was that a good time in your life? Many people do not have fond memories of middle school or high school. It's an awkward time for most of us, trying to figure out who we are, how we are, what we're good at, and what we're not. Bodies and hormones are changing and we're constantly comparing ourselves with others. That's normal. At the same time we were comparing ourselves, we were also trying to figure out what was unique and valuable about ourselves. This is a time of identity formation. But in many cases, the first phase of identity formation, ironically, is borrowing identity from others. Kids are so in need of acceptance and belonging from their peers that they often follow the fashions and habits of others. Wearing the same style of clothes, and enjoying or experimenting with the same things as their group, gives them a start at forming an identity. In middle and high school, I had a choice of which group to identify with: the greasers, the nerds or intellectuals, the surfers, the social cliques, or the jocks. Remember those? I decided on the surfer uniform of that period: a Pendleton shirt on top of a white t-shirt, white Levis, and white low-top tennis shoes. Don't ask me why – I guess I thought that was cool.

The ideal in Western cultures is to eventually form an individual identity. This may not be true in other parts of the world. For Erikson, by the time you're 18 years old, you ought to have some idea of who you are and what your role will be in life.

Perhaps in 1950 when his book first came out, it seemed reasonable for Erikson to imagine that young people were eager to become adults. Is that still true today – are the myriad of career paths open to young people in the 21st century good news or confusing news? More young adults are living at home for longer periods of time, in what's called "failure to launch." It may be that they haven't finished growing up or are confused by the many options for identity afforded them. I had a client years ago whose husband was virtually never home. He played golf and drank with his buddies many times a week. Relationally, he was still in middle school.

Intimacy vs. Isolation (18-40 years old)

From 18 to 40, in Erikson's mind, was a time to find a life partner and form an intimate bond. This, too, may be different in the 21st century. People are making other choices, not necessarily marrying early in life or at all. But intimacy can be found in other ways besides marriage or romantic relationships. It's possible to find intimate friendships and intimate family connections. The idea is not to be afraid of intimacy. One definition of intimacy is "close familiarity."

As I shared earlier, Dr. Vivek Murthy wrote in his 2020 book *Together* that human beings are hardwired for connection. He also wrote that isolation frequently leads to stress-related physical illnesses, depression, and even suicide. So, if you're not married or in a romantic relationship, find a close friend or friends with whom you can develop closeness, trust, and intimacy. It might save your life. It will certainly improve it.

Generativity vs. Stagnation (40-65 years old)

Generativity often means transcending your own interests in order to provide care for others. It can also mean being creative, generating new business, creative ideas, raising a family, or running a company. It can even mean finding an enjoyable pastime that gives back a sense of accomplishment. If we aren't being generative in some way, if we don't have a way to give of ourselves in some meaningful way, we may end up stagnating.

I was alarmed at how my uncle deteriorated after his retirement. His wife, my aunt, passed away a few years previously, and after mandatory retirement from his work, he sat in front of the television all day, stagnating. I found myself writing a poem titled "I Saw a Dead Man Today" and wondered in the poem when did he die – was it when his children moved away, when his wife died, when he retired? Some people die slowly, when the meaning and focus of their lives are gone. In a later chapter, I write about having a good death versus a bad death. To stay alive and to have a good death, it's important to invest in someone or something in a meaningful way. It's important to find a source and focus for giving back – for generativity.

Too many retired people or people who have invested their identity in various roles become stuck. They haven't developed enough meaningful interests to sustain them after they are no longer needed to function in a role. You may live well past the age where you will be needed by an employer, by a spouse, or by your children. What will you do? Where will you find meaning and a life-giving, life-enhancing pastime?

That is rarely a problem in Italy. We have family there that we visit at least two months out of each year. The custom in Italy, as it is in many other countries around the world, is for the grandparents to continue to be closely involved in the lives of their grandchildren. In fact, on a busy street near our apartment in Sarnaco, there's a yellow caution sign with the outline of an older person with a walking cane leading a youngster by the hand. We see Nonnos and Nonnas regularly walking kids to school. Generativity, the enjoyment (or need) for giving back, participating in family life, or helping out in the community or place of worship, is a very good source of life-long generativity.

Integrity vs. Despair (65+ years old)

Reader, this is likely the developmental stage you're in. Among the developmental tasks that correspond to this stage include reflecting on one's life and developing a point of view about death. Integrity, as I have said earlier, does not refer to character but to quality. If you've reached the stage of integrity, it means that you can reflect on your life, hopefully knowing that it was meaningful and well-lived.

The negative pole of this developmental stage is called "despair." It's unfortunate that so many older people finish their journey full of regrets. Reflecting back on bad decisions, missed opportunities, or unlived potentials can bring disappointments and heartache. In some cases, the disappointments create bitterness and deep despair. I can't imagine anyone looking back at their lives without some regrets or disappointments. However, it may be that you can transform some or all of your disappointments by realizing that it isn't too late to make amends in some cases, or to use the remaining time you have left to live to make a difference in the lives of others. As Gene Cohen has written in *The Mature Mind*, your mind is still growing and developing even in later years. There are some distinct advantages of having been around awhile. One of the vital resources of older adults is wisdom, the wisdom that may be passed on, or the wisdom and perspective about life that can simply be savored.

Development in Later Years

I shared earlier that Cohen divides human development from midlife on into four phases: phase I: from early forties to late fifties; phase II: from late fifties to early seventies; phase III: late sixties through the eighties; and phase IV: from late seventies to the end of life. Erikson didn't have as much to say about developmental stages in the later part of life. However, now that people on average are living longer and there is increased understanding about the workings of the brain such as neuroplasticity and neurogenesis, it makes sense that many older adults can look forward to the potential of a rich final journey.

Let's look at these stages in more depth. We'll begin with the classic midlife reevaluation (some folks call it a crisis, but it doesn't have to be). Midlife is often a time of change and change can feel unwelcome. However, understanding, accepting, and preparing for midlife will help to avoid the feeling of crisis.

Phase I, *midlife reevaluation*, can begin as early as the age of thirty-five, but it's more common from the early forties to late fifties. This stage, Cohen writes, is characterized by *reevaluation*, *exploration*, and *transition*. This could actually be a crisis if you are tired of the life you have lived so far and feel stuck. Perhaps you truly are stuck. It isn't easy to leave a job you dislike or are tired of doing. Maybe you think "At my age…" or "I have to support my family" or "It's too late for me to retrain" or "I'm better off staying where I am." If that's the case, I have some suggestions for you. Using Cohen's terms, they have to do with exploration and transition. I'll explain later in this chapter.

Phase II, Cohen says, is about *liberation*, *experimentation*, and *innovation*. Liberation happens because in your mid-fifties to mid-seventies, you are less interested in having to impress people. You are, hopefully, more self-accepting and have an easier time speaking your mind. Of course, if you are retired or semi-retired, you also have more choices available for how to spend your time. That is truly liberating.

When I was 40, I remember barbecuing a steak on the patio of my suburban home with two cars in the garage and a daughter playing in the yard and thinking to myself how fortunate I was to be at this stage of life. My next thought was, I've done what I'm supposed to have done, I have met all of my parental and societal requirements, now I can do a little more of what I enjoy doing. It was a nice thought but because I had a very demanding occupation, it was only a nice thought. Cohen thinks that the liberation that comes with an older person is mostly a felt sense of "internal liberation." I did feel more liberated in the sense that, having done what I was supposed to do, now I could continue to do what I had been doing because *I chose to do it*. I asked a friend recently if he had noticed a difference in himself now that he is semi-retired and only working the hours he wants. "Freedom," he said, "a real sense of freedom." Cohen's second phase immediately came to mind.

In addition to liberation, Cohen speaks of experimentation and innovation. That makes sense. If you are more self-accepting and feel freer to try new things, you can experiment. You can try things and not worry so much that you won't be very good at them. One of my older students named Susan cried when I handed back her midterm. She hadn't expected to get an A. In fact, she wasn't even sure that at her advanced age, she should even be in graduate school. "You can do this," I reminded her quietly. So she did – graduating with a master's degree in psychology with an emphasis in marital and family therapy. I love teaching older students. Like Susan, many of them are unsure about going back to school. They've raised children, had a career, experienced life, and know that there is still more to do. Older adults often make excellent students. In some cases, they have fewer life burdens to carry, but in all cases, they are eager to continue challenging themselves and growing. They frequently also make excellent therapists. They have lived life and acquired wisdom and very little surprises them, so they are more self-accepting and accepting of others – just as Maslow predicted. But, of course, going back to school is only one of so many things that older people can plunge into.

Phase III, between the late sixties and early eighties, is a time for *recapitulation, resolution,* and *contribution*. You don't see the word "recapitulation" very often. The Oxford Dictionary defines recapitulation as "an act or instance of summarizing and restating the main points of something. In biology recapitulation is the repetition of an evolutionary or other process during development or growth. In music, it's the part of a movement (especially one in sonata form) in which themes from the exposition are restated." Cohen appears to be saying that at this age we are reviewing, perhaps reworking experience, memory, and values – what still makes sense, what's important to remember, and what's important to hold on to.

I wonder if that has to do with the overflowing memories that many older people experience. For many of us, long-term memory continues into old age while short-term memory sometimes declines. Reviewing and reworking what has been important is a good thing when you finally feel a bit more liberated from meeting external obligations. Liberated or not, a lifetime of memories invites sorting through and reflecting on one's life. Some aspects of life, especially relationships, can hopefully be resolved and repaired. Mental and emotional energy may be freed and opened up to find meaningful ways to make a contribution.

Phase IV, from the late seventies to the end of life, is a time of *continuation, reflection,* and *celebration.* I'll drink to that! At 73, I continue to enjoy my family and friends. I enjoy my hobbies and pastimes, and with luck, I'll continue to stay healthy. Overflowing memories at our age make it hard not to reflect back on life. Many of us are asking, "How did I do?" or "How am I doing?" We may also be asking, "What is left to do?" It's good to reflect on your life, to repair, if you're able, as many of the bad decisions and hurts that you caused, and to celebrate the good decisions and love that you have shared.

Looking Inward

Now that we've looked at the Erickson's stages of life and Cohen's stages of midlife and beyond, let's turn to C.G. Jung, a famously sought-after psychiatrist in Switzerland in the first half of the 20th century. In his 1955 book *Modern Man in Search of a Soul*, Jung made an interesting statement.

> I have treated many hundreds of patients, the larger number being Protestants, a smaller number Jews, and not more than five or six believing Catholics. Among all my patients in the second half of life - that is to say over thirty-five - there has not been one whose problem in the last resort was not that of finding a religious outlook on life. It is safe to say that every one of them fell ill because he had lost that which the living religions of every age have given to their followers, and not one of them has really healed who did not regain his religious outlook.

In other words, Jung is saying that having faith is an important source of meaning in life. In that same book, Jung said that life can be thought of as the arc of a projectile – coming into life, reaching a zenith of ego development around midlife, and then turning back down toward eventual death. A transformation occurs around midlife when a healthy individual is less interested in the requirements and benefits of the outer world and begins to look inward toward what Jung called the "Self." In Jungian language, the Self is an internal blueprint for whom you're supposed to be or become. As I mentioned above, we don't always choose what we are interested in, especially in the first half of life. Certain things appeal to us and other things, not so much. Why is that? One explanation has to do with our upbringing. We might have been exposed to something that wasn't intrinsically interesting to us, but because we were taught its value, we cultivated an interest over time. But, sometimes, even in early life, we discover our own individual interests and direction, and we somehow know that this is the direction we want to take our lives.

In his 1996 book *The Soul's Code: In Search of Character and Calling*, James Hillman wrote about people who knew at a young age who they were and what work they wanted to do in their life. Hillman thought to title his book "the acorn theory." He wanted to emphasize that everything that is an oak is present in the acorn – by extension, the adult we are to become is present in the child. The title was changed to *The Soul's Code* partly because people are more interested in souls than in acorns. Also, Hillman knew that the "code" or blueprint for whom we are intended to become while residing in our spirit is communicated and experienced in our soul and fleshed out in our biology.

Jung wrote that the process of "individuation" is a journey to become a whole individual – in Hillman's language, to individuate is to grow from an acorn into the oak we are meant to be. Similar to Maslow's ideas, a "whole," self-actualized person is someone who has done the hard work of finding a fit, a confluence, between who one is and what one does. The self-actualized or individuated person is conscious of imperfections, and failings, yet is self-accepting and accepting of others. This person has become wise, gracious, and loving. The work of individuation is the midlife challenge of looking within, being less concerned about externals and more focused on becoming the "self" (the oak) that God or nature intended.

The term "whole" doesn't mean perfect. It means, "I have a pretty good idea of who I am and why I'm here." Whole, in the way we're describing it here, doesn't mean "done." Actually, it could mean "ready." "I know who I am and why I'm here so I can relax and continue to *enjoy* the work I'm here to do – and maybe there is more interesting work ahead. I'm ready!"

Your journey thus far has been about learning what's important in life, what's important to you. If there is still more to learn, good, you're not done yet. Your life up to this point has presented you with opportunities to learn and to love. As you reflect, you may notice the times that you got off the path and what brought you back when you felt confused or lost. But now here you are. You have learned a lot. You have helped others on their journey. It's likely that you can say that it worked out pretty well. You can also ask yourself, "What's next?" Because you're not done living yet.

CHAPTER 3

———————— • ————————

SO, WHAT'S YOUR STORY?

The way we imagine our lives is the way we are going to go on living our lives. For the manner in which we tell ourselves about what is going on is the genre through which events become experiences.

~James Hillman, *Healing Fiction*

You Live Inside a Story

You probably don't realize that you are living a hero's journey. Everyone is. As you think about your life, you realize that your story contains many of the same sorts of choices and challenges that people have always had to face - some more, some less. I don't imagine that anyone thinks of themselves as a hero or heroine. Popular film and literature have elevated that concept to a small group of people who stand out for their courage or contribution. Of course, we do celebrate those amazing souls who step up in a crisis, whether a crisis of imminent or ongoing danger to human life. Have you shown courage? Have you made a contribution? Answer that question, not from a newspaper headline, nor a movie-goer's perspective, but from God's perspective. You may see things differently.

First, let's look at your story from the standpoint of the classic hero's journey in mythology. Probably no one knew more about mythic journeys than Joseph Campbell, the one who wrote *The Hero with a*

Thousand Faces. Campbell read hero's journey stories from hundreds of cultures from around the world across different time periods. He collected those stories, analyzing the common themes and archetypal patterns from one story to the next, and compiled the basic outline of the hero's journey.

The hero's journey is your journey. Whether or not you feel like one, you are the hero or heroine of your own story. Dan McAdams wrote a book called *The Stories We Live By*. McAdams wrote that people tend to think of their life as a story, and that makes sense because our brain is a natural storyteller. Brains categorize experience into story-form in order to make sense of life, to create some continuity, predictability, and the ability to anticipate and plan for the future. Some brains don't like thinking about the future and others are obsessed with it. Healthy people discipline their brains to strike a balance between thinking and planning for the future but not obsessing about it. The psychologist Dan Siegel said that brains "narrativize" experience in order to create autobiographical memory. Autobiographical memory is what gives you a sense of your identity and continuity in your life.

So, apparently, we live inside of the stories that our brains create, for better or worse. The homes and cultures we grow up in and the families that raise us create the context in which our story begins. McAdams writes, "By the time each of us reaches adolescence and adulthood, we are ready to create stories of a certain type. By the time we think seriously about the meaning of our own lives, we may already be predisposed to create that meaning through the filtering glass of tragedy, comedy, irony, or romance." What stories have you created of your life?

Story Genres

Simplistically, in a *tragic* story the action seems to run away with the plot and people make poor and often irreversible decisions. In a *comic* story, the action proceeds more slowly and people make mistakes but are able to recover and even laugh at themselves. An *ironic story* is one in which what is expected differs radically from what actually happens.

That's a favorite vehicle for producers of action movies. Then, of course, *romance* is about the ups and downs of love. Another story genre is called the "epic." An *epic* genre is about a hero or heroine and their quests and adventures. The hero's journey is an example of an epic genre. Probably the most famous epic journey in recent film is the *Lord of the Rings* trilogy. The hero has a task that requires courage and help from others. He faces challenges and adversities and completes the task of protecting Middle Earth from evil.

Google "archetypes of the hero's journey" for more insight or watch the first *Star Wars* movie again. In that movie, as in the *Lord of the Rings*, you will find all of the elements and archetypes that were used to create a timeless story of a hero's journey. George Lucas was a huge fan of Joseph Campbell and consulted Campbell's book *The Hero with a Thousand Faces* for research into archetypal character development. The term "archetype" is used to describe consistent themes of human experience across time and geography. So, terms like hero, villain, quest, warrior, mentor and so forth are themes that one finds in stories from around the world. Archetypes are concepts and images that seem to be embedded in the human psyche. As a result, reading a book or viewing a movie that grips you does so because the images and action are already familiar to you at some level of consciousness.

Movies may be today's primary art form. It isn't surprising, then, that the movies we seem to like the most are about heroes and heroines. These films are the campfire stories that our ancestors thrilled at, stories that helped to guide them in discovering traditions and values. Robert McKee, who wrote *Story,* the screenwriter's bible, wrote that we go to the movies to discover who we are. If that is true, is there a movie that you can watch over and over again or a book that you've read and reread? Does that tell you something about your journey so far and, perhaps how you would like your journey to continue forward – your hero or heroine's journey? McKee's book suggests that we aren't just one of the characters in a movie but, in many ways, we are all of the characters. In the movies we love, we face again and again our challenges and our victories.

We don't have to go to the movies to see heroes and heroines. They are all around us, living their everyday lives with courage and stamina, quietly facing daily challenges and adversities. You are doing this as well, in terms of the major stages of the hero's journey. You left the familiar events and contexts of childhood and ventured out. You crossed common thresholds of education, employment, and relationships. You met allies and enemies, people who helped you, and people who hurt you. You faced ordeals, perhaps guided or inspired by a mentor, a favorite teacher, a coach, or a family member, and here you are. What have you learned? Has your life worked out the way you wanted it to? It's worth thinking about and asking yourself these questions.

For those interested in reading more about the heroine's journey, read Maureen Murdock's *The Heroine's Journey*; Samantha Ellis' *How to Be a Heroine*; and Esther Harding's *The Way of All Women*. All of these authors explore the myths and literature of a woman's journey. There are many common elements to the hero and heroine's journey, but a woman may experience her journey very differently than a man. She has a different experience of her body, her place in her family, and in her position in society. As a woman, consider what you have had to face and the challenges you have met. Your heroine's journey may have taken you far afield into the realms of social, educational, or financial achievement. Your heroine's journey may have been the constancy of your devotion to your family, your children, your grandchildren, your place of worship, your career or your community. How would you characterize your journey so far?

In Chapter 1, we discussed the value of having a map, a guide, and a compass. In addition, we discussed what to take with you, what to leave behind, and what to do while you're still here. Finally, we discussed the idea of a soul and the value of love. In Chapter 2, we discussed the first part of your journey from childhood onward, and emphasized the journey from the second half of life and beyond. In this present chapter, we'll continue to look ahead - where you are, and where you're headed. It's good to realize that you are living a story. In fact, you are the author of that story; you are the hero or heroine on your journey.

How Else to Prepare for Your Journey Ahead

What else do you need to do while you're still here? Of course, I don't need to suggest doing whatever it takes to stay healthy. There are plenty of books, magazines, and online articles about that. One book I especially like is the 2002 book *Aging with Grace: What the Nun Study Teaches Us About Leading Longer, Healthier, and More Meaningful Lives.* The nuns in the study lived, ate, and worked together – a perfect environment for a controlled study of the effects of Alzheimer's disease on the brain. The nuns who were able to avoid developing Alzheimer's (according to annual cognitive and physical function evaluations during old age, and postmortem neuropathologic evaluations of their brains) remained active – reading, writing letters, doing crossword puzzles, and other pastimes to keep their brains active. I also like Daniel Amen's *Stones of Remembrance: Healing Scriptures for Your Mind, Body, and Soul,* published in 2017. There are many other good books on how to keep your brain and body functioning well while you're on your journey.

As far as I know, I have only one thing in common with Bill Gates. We both travel with books. I like reading about how to stay healthy while I'm still able. I also like to read about what to expect in the next life. Of course, no one knows for sure but there are some folks who report having been there. I don't know what to believe about that, but it does make fascinating reading. Kelly Bulkeley and Dr. Patricia Bulkley wrote *Dreaming Beyond Death: A Guide to Pre-Dreams and Visions.* Dr. Bulkley was a spiritual services provider for hospice for ten years. She recorded many of the dreams reported by patients who were in the process of letting go of this life. The interesting thing about these dreams is that they often placed the dreamer in a transitional space, like a waiting room. Is our earthly life a "transitional space?" Throughout this book, I'll keep listing a few of books that I've appreciated, but here's my larger point about reading these books: this is going to be an amazing adventure. Don't you want to learn as much as you can about where you're headed? Hopefully, you also want to learn the best way to genuinely enjoy your journey.

Life's Labyrinth

Below is an image of a labyrinth, like the famous one on the floor of Chartres Cathedral in France. Do you know the difference between a labyrinth and a maze? Most people don't. If you look closely at the image below, you'll notice that, unlike a maze, a labyrinth has no dead ends or wrong turns. Once you enter the labyrinth, if you are patient and consistent, you will get to the center. Like life, your journey will not be linear. Walking the Labyrinth, much of the time it seems as if you're going the wrong direction; much of the time you seem to be going around in circles. A maze, on the other hand, is for entertainment - if you don't get too frustrated with lots of wrong turns and dead ends trying to find your way through it (I guess that's like life also).

A labyrinth is for spiritual growth. Walking the labyrinth requires patience and faith that, despite appearances, you will get to the center. The labyrinth is designed for you to visit four different quadrants. I think the ancients envisioned the world that way. The labyrinth teaches us about life and if we take the time as we walk, we learn about ourselves.

It's very easy to forget what is important in life and get caught up in the blur of activity. My wife and I were walking a labyrinth made of stones in a large garden near San Luis Obispo, California. We walked slowly, enjoying the garden and the evening air. Some young people joined us. Starting their journey, they quickly became bored and hopped over the rings of stones to the center of the labyrinth. "Yay!" they cried and moved on. "That's so California," I thought. "Just get to your goal the quickest possible way." Or, maybe that's true of youth everywhere. Of course, they missed the lesson. Among the many lessons that can be learned, walking the labyrinth is the value of patiently enjoying the journey. Try Googling "labyrinth near me" and see if you can find one to walk as you contemplate your life's journey.

Life Lessons

What lessons have you learned? If you wrote down everything that life has taught you, it would be a long list. Wouldn't it be nice if you could give your list to a young person and have them truly benefit from it? Good luck with that. We older folks have been passing down our lessons and wisdom to young people from the beginning of time. Maybe some of it gets in, but youth have always wanted to learn their own lessons. It was probably true with us as well. What was the most important lesson you learned in your life? Is there someone you could share that lesson with? I wonder how many of our life lessons would be similar. It seems that most belief systems value learning life's lessons and being responsible for the choices we make.

Interestingly, it seems that in some belief systems, our choices may even predate our birth. Sobonfu Somé was a member of the Dagara tribe of West Africa. She wrote *Welcoming Spirit Home*, published in 1999. She wrote that the Dagara people believe that we choose when and to whom we are born. She wrote, "If we view reality from the angle that we come to earth to fulfill a particular purpose, birth can then be looked at as a contract between this world and the world of the ancestors or other dimensions…. If we believe that our greatest wounds (and choices) are in fact our greatest gifts, we can embrace the idea that the hardships we experience in our families of origin are no accidents." What do you think of that? I'm not sure how widely that idea is accepted, but it is interesting. Many belief systems endorse the idea that our spirit inhabits eternity and takes on an earthly body in order to achieve particular tasks or learn important lessons.

My Christian background doesn't have much to say about that except for the belief that we have always been *intentional*. Christians believe that God not only created us, but also has given us the ability to respond to Him, and has given us a purpose for our life. We can choose to accept our purpose and thus make sense and find the meaning of our life - or not. It's our choice. However, beyond discovering our own individual sense of purpose, the larger purpose of life, according to Christian belief, is to experience God's love and to become more successful at becoming a loving person. What we learn in life may relate, somehow, to how we experience eternity. It's interesting to me that the choices people make in this life seem to factor into other religions as well. Let's look at the Islamic, Jewish, and Christian religions a little more closely. As you read about them, see how they correspond to your own beliefs.

The Islamic Religion

I had a conversation with a Muslim Imam at a local Islamic Center to find out what they believe. Here is what that Imam told me about the purpose of life, their burial customs, and the fate of the soul in the afterlife.

Life's Purpose in Islam

According to the Quran found in Surah 67, life and death are given by Allah, and no one else can grant life or cause death. The object of giving life and causing death is to test humans to see if they choose good deeds or bad deeds. The results of these choices will determine a human's fate in the afterlife. Although Allah is all-powerful, He is also merciful and forgiving, not tyrannical and cruel. With repentance and forgiveness, a believer can expect to go to heaven. There are seven heavens in Islam. Believers are granted access to levels of heaven according to their deeds.

Burial Customs in Islam

These may vary somewhat according to cultural customs, but typically, the body of the deceased is buried as soon as possible. Because the dignity of the body is respected, individuals are buried and not cremated. The body of the deceased is carefully washed and placed in a shroud, and carried without a coffin to the place of burial. Coffins are permitted when required by local law. The idea is that mourners have direct contact with the body of the deceased to be ever more mindful of life's certain end. The simple burial confirms the belief that from earth we were made and to earth we will return.

The Fate of the Soul in Islam

This is determined by one's life on earth. Two angels appear to review the deeds done on earth. An angel of compassion and an angel of righteousness will accompany the soul to Barzakh, a transitional waiting space prior to the judgment of Allah. The arms of Allah are open to everyone who repents of their sins and turns to worship and obey Him. "Do not despair of Allah's mercy; whatever you might have done in the past, if you sincerely turn to your Lord's obedience, you will be forgiven every sin" (*Toward Understanding the Quran*, Sura 39:71).

The Jewish Religion

"People of the Book" is the term used in Islam for people of the Jewish and Christian faiths. Muslims acknowledge the holy men of the Torah and the Bible - Abraham, Moses, and Jesus are valued prophets. In Islam, Muhammad is the final prophet of God.

I also spoke with a local Rabbi about these same issues from a Jewish perspective. I learned that Jewish traditions may vary considerably depending on one's orientation, whether orthodox, conservative, or reformed. The distinction the Rabbi made is how strictly believers adhere to Jewish law and traditions.

Life's Purpose in Judaism

I found this wonderful summation of the life purpose in Judaism by Rabbi Lewis Eron in *Reconstructing Judaism* (2021). "The goal of Jewish life is to embody Torah, the living word of the living God addressed to all creation through the life and experience of Am Yisrael, the Jewish people. This Jewish insight teaches us that as Jews, we have the opportunity to take the wisdom of our tradition and make it real in the world in which we live. What we say and what we do is consequential. By making the spiritual and ethical insights of our Torah the foundation of our lives, we transcend our human limits. We connect ourselves to God, and can join our people's prophets, priests, kings, heroes and sages as one of those who live and teach Torah."

Burial Customs in Judaism

Burial services, interestingly, closely resemble those of the Islamic community. When a person dies, the body is washed and placed in a shroud - simple unadorned caskets are permitted. Cremation or embalming are not practiced. Burial takes place as soon as possible. Traditions vary on how long the period of mourning may be, from one afternoon to the more traditional seven days.

The Fate of the Soul in Judaism

The Rabbi emphasized that the practice of Judaism focuses more on what one does rather than on what one believes. This allows for some flexibility and diversity in beliefs. Jewish people believe in the divine nature of a human being; thus, many believe in the immortality of the soul. In addition, many Jews believe in the resurrection of the physical body, joining with the soul at the advent of the Messiah. After death, a person's soul is assigned to a place of waiting until the advent of the messianic age when all souls will be resurrected to eternal life.

The Christian Religion

I discussed Christianity a little bit above, but let's go into more depth here for the purposes of comparison.

The Purpose of Life in Christianity

What is the purpose of life for Christians? It's likely that you will get different answers from the Christians you ask depending on their background and family of faith. A group of clerics and delegates from various churches in England and Scotland got together in the mid-1600s to come up with a simple unifying statement of faith. The Westminster Shorter Catechism was the result: "What is the chief end of man? The chief end of man is to glorify God and enjoy Him forever." The clerics were confident that this simple statement of faith would be adequate to serve as a unifying statement of belief for the Christian churches in the United Kingdom. There are many ways to glorify God and many ways to enjoy Him, but the simplicity of that statement, in my view, is the core message of the Gospel. The heart of the Christian life is to embody gratitude for God's gifts and grace.

Burial Customs in Christianity

I recently purchased a gravesite in the local cemetery. It cost $13,324, which seemed to be reasonable in the area where I live. I'm able to pay for it over time, interest-free. With luck and self-care, I shouldn't need it for a while. Why am I doing this? I ask myself. Why don't I simply join my wife in her Neptune Society burial at sea, which only costs about $1300? I don't know the answer to my question. Is it because of the traditional burial practices for Christians in this country, where we are placed in a coffin and buried in a cemetery with a stone or brass marker etched with the dates of birth and death and occasional family endearments? My father and mother were buried in the traditional way and, as far as I know, so were all of my relatives on both sides of my family. Is that the reason? Am I simply following tradition, or is it my vanity? Do I expect someone to visit my grave when I'm gone? I really don't know.

I picked out a gravesite in the local cemetery and found a nice spot under an oak tree. That wasn't too difficult living in a city called Thousand Oaks. I've met my neighbors. My spot is next to a couple who were married for many years. Next to them lies a woman who died much too early and near her is the grave of a little boy. Life can be so incredibly sad. Perhaps I made my decision because when I think ahead to the end of my life journey, I would like to picture my peaceful spot in the shade of an old oak. But is that worth $13,324?

Why is anyone buried or placed in a vault, chamber, or pyramid? The tradition goes back thousands of years. It isn't simply to prevent the indignity of being eaten by wild animals - I think there is much more to it than that. It may be that human beings recognize that life is precious and needs to be honored with a grave site that says the individual who lies here lived for a time on the earth. It may have been a long life or a short life, but it was a life, and life is precious.

As a Christian, and as my grandmother quipped, "You know that I'm not really going to be there," I know that I'm not going to be in that shady spot under an oak in a local cemetery, so why bother being buried? It may simply be a recognition that I lived here on earth for a time. I was born in 1949, four years after the end of World War II, and lived to be... well, we'll find out. But I will no longer be here - I'll be in eternity. I will have awakened from the dream that is life and I will be home.

The Fate of the Soul in Christianity

Christians believe they have an eternal soul that, after death, will join with God. Christians also believe that it is essential to embrace the saving, redemptive work of Jesus Christ made possible by his death and resurrection.

What's Important

It seems that Islam, Judaism, and Christianity, the three major Western religions, all agree on the sanctity of human life, the value of being responsive to God and to other human beings. The purpose of life is to learn about the value and centrality of love, to learn responsible behavior toward the earth, and to learn the value of one's fellow human beings. Obeying the commandments of God and the prompting of His spirit is what is important in life and what is essential for preparing for the life hereafter.

I don't know very much about the myriad of religious expressions in Eastern religions. It seems, from my limited experience, that Eastern religions also instruct adherents about the value of human life and the importance of faith and responsible behavior. I wonder if there is something in the human soul, regardless of our many different beliefs, that responds to an inner voice or awareness that one's life and the life of others have sacred significance and how we treat each other may have eternal consequences.

"Belief consists in accepting the affirmations of the soul."
~Ralph Waldo Emerson

Whether you like Sobonfu Somé's beliefs or the beliefs of the Imam, Rabbi, Christian Pastor or other faiths, the belief that your life is intentional is a very good thing to embrace. In fact, I think it's among the most important beliefs in life. Do you remember reading "Desiderata" by Max Ehrmann, which he copyrighted in 1927? I was in college in the 70s the last time I heard it read over the radio.

Desiderata (Things Desired)

Go placidly amid the noise and the haste, and remember what peace there may be in silence. As far as possible, without surrender, be on good terms with all persons.

Speak your truth quietly and clearly; and listen to others, even to the dull and the ignorant; they too have their story.

Avoid loud and aggressive persons; they are vexatious to the spirit. If you compare yourself with others, you may become vain or bitter, for always there will be greater and lesser persons than yourself.

Enjoy your achievements as well as your plans. Keep interested in your own career, however humble; it is a real possession in the changing fortunes of time.

Exercise caution in your business affairs, for the world is full of trickery. But let this not blind you to what virtue there is; many persons strive for high ideals, and everywhere life is full of heroism.

Be yourself. Especially do not feign affection. Neither be cynical about love; for in the face of all aridity and disenchantment, it is as perennial as the grass.

Take kindly the counsel of the years, gracefully surrendering the things of youth.

Nurture strength of spirit to shield you in sudden misfortune. But do not distress yourself with dark imaginings. Many fears are born of fatigue and loneliness.

Beyond a wholesome discipline, be gentle with yourself. You are a child of the universe no less than the trees and the stars; you have a right to be here.

And whether or not it is clear to you, no doubt the universe is unfolding as it should. Therefore be at peace with God, whatever you conceive Him to be. And whatever your labors and aspirations, in the noisy confusion of life, keep peace in your soul. With all its sham, drudgery and broken dreams, it is still a beautiful world. Be cheerful. Strive to be happy.

The beautiful sentiment above is all about choices - good choices, I would say. How are you doing? Have you made some of these choices? You'll hear me repeat this message throughout the book: it isn't too late.

I love my own faith tradition for all of the meaningful paths and practices it provides. But I want to encourage you on your own journey, your hero's or heroine's journey. Your life has value - that's the story. The point of this book is to encourage you to pay attention to your life, to your heroic journey. Because your life is valuable, it's important to take care of it. It follows that when you are taking care of your own life, you are also, directly or indirectly, taking care of the lives of others. In a brutal Nazi concentration camp, Vicktor Frankl made the decision to find meaning and purpose in his hellish journey. He found a reason to live in caring for other prisoners, comforting and encouraging them, and even feeding them morsels from his own plate. He said in his 1946 book, *Man's Search for Meaning,* that although he didn't have a choice not to suffer, he could, nonetheless, choose to suffer in an honorable way. He valued his own life, and, because of that, he has become a hero to others, then and now.

CHAPTER 4

HELP ALONG THE WAY

Does the road wind up-hill all the way?
Yes, to the very end.
Will the day's journey take the whole long day?
From morn to night, my friend.

~Christina Georgina Rossetti

An Uphill Journey

At times the journey takes us into some rough terrain, into places that are difficult to navigate. It's hard, at times, not to feel frustrated, fearful, or lost. Which path to take? Where will it lead? Why does this have to be so hard? We can't always hold on to a positive outlook. The journey of life can wear us down, especially when we're older. Our bodies don't work as well. Memory fails. We don't always like what we see in the mirror. We may feel frail. It's hard to do some of the things we used to enjoy doing. It's even harder for some - the ones who are filled with regrets - questions such as why didn't I, why did I, why me? It's rare to find a human being who doesn't have some regrets - regrets about the choices they've made or didn't make, regrets about lost opportunities and unlived life. It's easy to get depressed. We know we should try, but it's hard to stay positive about our life. Science has confirmed that having a positive outlook on life promotes psychological well-being and even the possibility of improved physical health. We know all that. But knowing it doesn't make it easier. How do I stay positive when it feels like it's all uphill from here.

Should we even be thinking about our life's end? Is trying to stay positive or coming to terms and preparing for death a bad idea – can it promote a harmful negative outlook? Should I not have bothered writing this book? What about you? Would you prefer to stay positive and hopeful about your life, until circumstances force you to face your mortality? Or do you want to feel prepared? If you bought this book for yourself, you're clearly wanting to feel prepared. If someone else bought it for you and you're reading it reluctantly, that may be less true.

For me, these are not rhetorical questions. I don't have clear answers. In this respect my Christian faith actually seems to complicate things. Jesus talked about the power of faith – moving mountains and so forth. In fact, throughout Scripture, people are encouraged to have faith that God is good and desires only good, and that faith will work to confirm that "God works all things together for good." But for who's good – God's good, my good, other people's good, for who's good are all things being worked out? Are we just supposed to trust that some good will come out of whatever awful stuff we're going through?

C.S. Lewis asked similar questions in his books *The Problem of Pain* (1940) and especially in *A Grief Observed* (1961) in which he takes God to task, angrily expressing his grief and disillusionment over the death of his wife, Joy. You get a brief look at this in the movie *Shadowlands*, where Anthony Hopkins plays the part of Lewis. In the film, we see Lewis's excruciating torment and doubts about any meaning behind his terrible loss of his wife. The film ends without showing us any resolution nor the rekindling of Lewis' faith. To see that, you have to travel through the torment with Lewis as he writes in his journal, later published as *A Grief Observed*. Lewis, an Oxford Don, found the Christian faith late in life and became an important speaker, writer, and apologist for the belief in Jesus Christ. Regardless of the strength of one's faith, however, there are times of trial and doubt. *In a Grief Observed*, Lewis allows his intense grief, confusion, and anger to flow into his journal –

a cathartic release of overwhelming emotion. Yet, in his journal, we also see Lewis' eventual renewal and restoration of his new understanding of God's grace. In one way or another, life is an uphill journey for all of us. We can only hope for help along the way.

Faith *For* Versus Faith *In*

I've seen, firsthand, many remarkable answers to prayer. So, it's hard for me to be agnostic about the efficacy of prayer. I do believe that one can and should ask for God's help in tough times. And sometimes I think that prayers should be specific. In the very conservative Christian circles that I'm familiar with, you are encouraged not to dilute the power of your faith with a "negative confession." This means that you don't say or infer anything that would seem to contradict your faith that God will work in a particular situation. In the extreme, it might be considered a lack of faith to see a doctor or take medicine. I think that's a mistake. Yes, I do think that it's possible to pray for a specific outcome. And, at times, I think we should. Scripture encourages us to trust God with our needs. No one knows why it seems that some specific prayers are answered and others are not (or not obviously). In those instances, I have to shift from having faith *for* a specific outcome to having faith *in* God - trusting in His love and omniscience. Is that a cop-out? Am I being too passive? Do I lack faith? Those are interesting questions that I'll explore in this chapter.

Truths in Tension

People have been struggling for generations trying to understand this: if God is omniscient and omnipotent, why does He permit sin and suffering? The psalmist, David, writes, "My tears fall into what I'm drinking. You were very angry with me. So you picked me up and threw me away" (Psalm 102). This is how it feels when you're suffering - that God, or the universe, must be angry with you. You feel useless and discarded. Of course, this is depression, and David gives us a good description of how people feel when they're depressed. But, later in that same Psalm, he talks about the goodness of God and how His goodness will be remembered by future generations.

So, which is it? Does God or the universe punish people and throw them away? Or is God or the universe benevolent and loving? What are we supposed to believe?

I like what Rabbi Harold Kushner has to say in *When Bad Things Happen to Good People*: "I no longer hold God responsible for illness, accidents, and natural disasters, because I realize that I gain little, and I lose so much when I blame God for those things. Does it make sense that God is not an active agent in human misfortune? Why do most people think that God is responsible for the bad things that happen to us?" In a similar vein, C.S. Lewis wrote in the *Problem of Pain*, "Try to exclude the possibility of suffering which the order of nature and the existence of free wills involve, and you find that you have excluded life itself." Both of these men had suffered personally. They had dwelled on, to excruciating lengths, the problem of pain and suffering and God. They concluded that God is not the problem.

I went through a difficult time in my own life where I was angry at God. As a therapist, I was witnessing human suffering on an hourly basis for many years. I was also experiencing my own personal pain. I didn't think God was doing a very good job of running the world. Where was the love I had heard about? Where was the benevolence and grace? I was attending an Episcopal church at the time. Above the altar was a very lifelike crucifix. As the choir sang softly off to one side, and the congregation was kneeling, I found myself quietly weeping. I realized at that moment that underneath my anger was pain. It's very hard to be angry at someone hanging on a cross. I felt a little embarrassed about my tears, but a voice inside said if you can't cry here, where can you cry? At that moment, I realized that life is painful for everyone, but that we do not have to suffer alone or without hope.

The truths in tension are that the world is messed up and human beings do their part to keep it that way. But all of our various faiths tell us that divine love also exists and that we can call on that love when we are suffering. What happens when we do? It's confusing. Sometimes it seems that God is active in answering prayer and sometimes it seems that we're on our own. People say that God always answers prayer. Sometimes the answer is yes and sometimes it's no. Added to this is the problem of what exactly to pray for and where the prayer is coming from. I once sensed this question rising up from the inside of me: "What prays louder, your lips or your heart?" I wonder. Some people suggest that praying is a way of putting yourself on alert, ready to see the answer to your prayer when it arrives. When I'm looking for some specific items at a swap meet or flea market, for example, I try to put in mind the three or four things I'm looking for. That way, I'll actually see them when I come across them in the myriad of other objects on display. I wonder if prayer works similarly.

I said earlier that wondering about where God is in the midst of human suffering is a good question to ponder. Like having something in mind to look for at a flea market, keeping this question in mind may help you to arrive at some sort of an answer – maybe even a good one. C.S. Lewis said that suffering is God's megaphone to rouse a deaf world. Maybe he's right. But pain is one hell of a megaphone. I would prefer a gentler nudge. Besides, I don't think that God needs a megaphone. The state of the world and how people treat each other is enough to rouse questions and emotions in all searching human beings.

Faith or Fatalism

The apostle James said that it's best not to say, "I will," but it's better to say "if God wills…." In this James is advocating humility. The equivalent saying in Islam, "Inshallah" (if God wills), is the humble acknowledgment that God has the ultimate say in our life. I believe that. But some people find the idea hard to grasp. Hanging on to faith can be hard. For some, it seems impossible. It may seem easier just to leave God out of the picture altogether and adopt an attitude of *que sera sera*. I can certainly appreciate that life's uphill journey and hard knocks can tire you out and wear you down. Where do you stand on that continuum between faith and fatalism?

Life can be unendurably hard. Some people face unimaginable suffering. I can understand why people give up. There are so many disappointments and disillusionments that make it difficult to hold onto any kind of faith in a benevolent universe. The awful paradox between the reality of suffering and believing in a knowing and loving God is often incomprehensible. In the face of this paradox, there may be numerous positions: "I can't believe in God," or "If there is a God, He or She doesn't seem to care about what's going on down here" or "I believe in God, but I sure don't understand His ways." This may be a more fatalistic way of saying, "If God wills."

I have a friend who went through a horribly painful time of mental anguish in college. Psychiatrists and medication helped but the mental pain continued to afflict her. She found relief and strength from an unexpected source, reading Vicktor Frankl's *Man's Search for Meaning*, where, as I mentioned in the last chapter, Frankl finds meaning in caring for others. After reading Frankl's account of his time in the concentration camp, my friend decided that she could face her trials as well. Frankl helped her to regain her faith in God and in the possibility of surviving her trauma and imagining a better future. It is so encouraging to read or listen to stories about people who have faced terrible hardship and trauma and found the will to live.

Some people are gifted. They are able to say, "If God wills" with genuine faith that in spite of human suffering, God does care. They believe that behind the scenes, God is at work - that there is sufficient evidence to hold on to faith. I like the tapestry metaphor. The back of the tapestry is a confusion of seemingly unconnected threads and patterns. Turn the tapestry around. Looking through the eyes of faith, life can make sense and even be beautiful. Through the eyes of faith, one can see the hand of God at work. Looking back, through the eyes of faith, one can say that it could have been much worse. Looking ahead, through the eyes of faith, one is able to say, "Things *will* be better."

I believe that there is help along the way. So, I pray every day, whether I'm in a good place or not. I pray for wisdom and guidance for my day. I pray for opportunities to offer a kind act or say a kind word. I thank God for what's been and what will be. I agree with Rabbi Kushner that it's better that I do. It's better for me to believe that God is present when things work out or, at least, that He is present regardless. It's better for my mental health and for my physical well-being. And, who knows, perhaps God is actually intimately interested and involved in our lives. Unless we are looking for it, we may not see His hand in the circumstances of our life.

Friends and Family

You may not see the hand of God or an answer to prayer as a miraculous, unmistakable event. Instead, God may be at work nudging a family member or friend to look in on you. It's astonishing how often someone calls right when they're needed. I have said and I've heard people say, "I was just about to call you!" "How did you know I needed some help?" It's certainly nice when that happens, but it may be that you are the one getting the nudge.

Have you ever had the feeling that you should call someone? I was driving home from my office one evening and a client I hadn't seen for years suddenly came to mind. I could see her face in my mind's eye and wondered why I thought of her. I said a brief prayer for her, as I often do when someone comes to mind, and I continued driving. Not an hour passed from the time I got home before my phone rang. Guess who it was? Her father had just passed away and she wanted to talk about it. You would think that those kinds of coincidences don't happen very often but, surprisingly, they do. I once asked a classroom of about 25 graduate students if any of them had a similar experience and nearly everyone raised their hand. In fact, I recall one class a few years ago when I asked that question and everyone raised their hand and even provided some amazing illustrations.

Rupert Sheldrake is a research scientist who has written extensively on these types of phenomena, what might be referred to as psychic experiences. Among his many books are *Dogs That Know When Their Owners Are Coming Home* (1999) and *The Sense of Being Stared At* (2011). Sheldrake, whose ideas and research have been dismissed by some as unscientific, does, however, make for fascinating reading. He thinks that it's possible to know more than we are consciously aware of – like when someone is staring at you or when someone is about to call, or you think of a song and it's suddenly on the radio. So, if you get a call from a family member or a close friend asking how you're doing, try to be open. Your friend or family member may know, better than you do, that there is something you may need to pay closer attention to.

Are you a person who is afraid to impose on others? My wife and I were children in the 50s. A strict social norm in those days was not to impose on anyone. I suppose that most people born in the mid-40s or early 50s have had similar training. While the idea of not imposing on people has value, it's not the supreme ethic. Sometimes it's a good idea to let people know that you'd like a little help. This may be especially true with family members. "Why didn't you call me?" is a question that is too frequently answered with, "I didn't want to impose." It's good to be considerate of your family and friends – considerate of their time, schedules, and other obligations. But it's also good to ask for help when you need it.

I think that most people like offering help. The exceptions would be when someone is constantly asking you for money, or not returning stuff they borrowed, or inviting themselves over and talking your ear off for hours. Some folks are much more needy than helpful. But in general, I do think people enjoy offering a helping hand on occasion. Ask yourself these questions: Do I try to avoid annoying people? Do I return what I've borrowed? Am I willing to offer help when asked? If the answer to these questions is yes, then don't be so worried about imposing, about asking for a bit of help when you need it. We all need help at times. We all need assistance with living.

Assisted Living

The term "assisted living" has taken on a specific meaning now as a particular place for the elderly or infirm to receive care. When it comes to caring for the elderly, Dr. Atul Gawande states in his 2017 book

Being Mortal that "in the main, the family has remained the primary alternative [to a live-in facility]. Your chances of avoiding the nursing home are directly related to the number of children you have and, according to what little research has been done, having at least one daughter seems to be crucial to the amount of help you will receive. But our greater longevity has coincided with an increased dependence of families on dual incomes, with results that are painful and unhappy for all involved."

It seems that as people age, they focus more on "being" rather than "doing," in part because they have retired from work, and in part because their bodies may not be able to do as much as they once could. A focus on being, on the quality of one's life, is one reason so many older adults prefer to live with family members where they feel connected. On Maslow's hierarchy of needs is "a sense of belongingness and love." Having previously achieved many of the earlier stages of Maslow's hierarchy, for many older folks, feeling a sense of connection and closeness becomes the highest priority. Gawande reports that contrary to what many people may think, "Older people reported more positive emotions as they age. They became less prone to anxiety, depression, and anger. They experience trials, to be sure, and more moments of poignancy – that is, of positive and negative emotion mixed together. But overall, they found living to be a more emotionally satisfying and stable experience as time passes, even as old age narrowed the lives they led."

I consider my younger brother a family hero. Like many aging adults, my father and mother preferred to remain at home as they grew more and more frail. Brian had retired and volunteered to move home to take care of them. Normally I would not recommend that family members feel the need and the pressure to take care of older adults. It can be difficult and often unpleasant work. Even though my parents gave him an allowance for their care, it was still much less expensive than in-home health care or a nursing home. It turned out that Brian was an excellent caregiver, patient and attentive. He saved the family a great deal of money. More importantly, he gave my parents the chance to be in familiar surroundings with family and friends nearby. But today, this is more of an exception – what's more common is that family members are simply unable, or unwilling, to provide the amount of care that older adults require.

Keren Brown Wilson had a great idea. She is credited with the development of the assisted living concept. In Volume 47 of *Gerontologist*, in December 2007, Dr. Brown traced the evolution of assisted living beginning in 1979. The key features of the assisted living concept are:

1. A residential-style physical environment, pertaining to (a) a resident's private space and (b) public community spaces shared by all residents.

2. A service capacity for (a) delivering routine services – both those amenable to being scheduled and those that could not be scheduled and (b) specialized health-related services.

3. An operating philosophy emphasizing resident choice and normal lifestyles related to (a) the governance of the resident's time, space, possessions, and contacts in his or her private space; and (b) decisions about accepting or rejecting medical care and other health-related care and services.

Some years ago, I visited my Aunt Mary in her apartment at an assisted living complex near Buffalo, New York. She had a fully furnished one-bedroom apartment including a kitchen where she could cook her own meals, as well as the means to communicate to the main office in case of an emergency. Down the hall was a common eating area where she could have all of her meals if she wished. I saw other older adults in a large living area playing cards or watching television. Aunt Mary introduced me to some of her friends. Her assisted living complex included three levels of care, from independent living, to assisted living, to full-time care including memory care. Thanks to Dr. Brown's idea, these types of assisted living facilities are all over the United States and in other countries around the world.

I visited Aunt Mary again recently. She is no longer capable of living independently and is in a skilled nursing facility. I was amazed at Aunt Mary's buoyant and joyful greeting. She looked great but, more importantly, she was genuinely happy. Mary is unable to walk on her own and has dementia. Although her memory is somewhat intact, she has difficulty forming sentences. I was reminded of Dr. Bruce Greyson's 2022 book, *After*. I'll discuss more of the book in another chapter. The point here is that Dr. Greyson, unlike other researchers, believes that the brain is a kind of filter, limiting what *could* be seen, heard, or felt, to what is necessary for living this life. The brain does not create the mind but is accessible to it. I'm guessing that if Aunt Mary's brain were fully functional, she would be more aware of her circumstances and less jubilant... just a thought. But I'm gratified that her spirit is very much alive, at peace, and genuinely happy.

When to Ask for Help

Life is an uphill journey. Or is it downhill? Of course, it's both. As we age, many things become more difficult. At the same time, we know that we are on the downward side of life. Life is difficult physically and emotionally. We need our family and friends to help us to feel alive and that we still have value. If we allow ourselves to feel as vulnerable as we truly are, our need for people to help can be a true blessing, the loving connections and support we need to face the final stretch of our journey.

When is it good to ask for help? Don't wait until you're feeling very depressed, even suicidal. That feeling usually comes and goes. Call someone. It never does any good to suffer in silence. My 79-year-old client has that feeling most mornings. After four years, he still misses his wife. He wonders why he is still here. Then he remembers the reason. He has friends and family who would miss him. He is involved in community service, and his faith prevents him from taking his own life. After coffee, he takes a long walk and feels much better afterward.

Don't be shy. Call on friends or family members when you feel down. It's easy for older adults to get depressed at times. That can be a normal response to the physical, emotional, and mental difficulties that challenge us as we get older. But sometimes, it's because you're worn down, emotionally exhausted, and your brain chemistry is off. You'd be surprised at how much better you might feel taking an anti-depressant to reboot your brain chemistry, if that's the problem. Your doctor may be able to prescribe something for you or recommend someone who can. Don't let yourself get too far down emotionally. Find someone to talk to. The same goes for you as a friend, family member, or caregiver. Be careful not to write off the moods of older adults just because they are older. You may need to talk to someone as well, for information or for your own mental health. You too can ask for help when you need it – when you're lonely, when you feel down or anxious, when you can't get around as easily, when you need a ride to the store or the doctor, when you need someone to talk to.

Speaking of which, I heartily recommend joining a group. There are basically four large categories of groups: therapy groups including grief groups; growth groups; support groups; and fun groups. If you're having a hard time letting go of a loved one, be sure to join a grief or bereavement group. They can be amazingly helpful in processing your loss. Over the years I've recommended grief groups to many people who were typically hesitant to go at first but were always glad they did. I wrote a book called *Growing Groups* in 2020 for a graduate group therapy class at Pepperdine University. In doing research for that book, I discovered that the largest number of groups fell into the support group category. You would be amazed at the number of support groups that are available. The groups include everything from new moms to empty nesters, and from support in taking care of the elderly, to being elderly. But you can also join a group simply for fun, for play-ing cards, knitting, crafts, baking, you name it. I still can't believe that my grandmother in her 80s was in a bowling league.

We all need help at times, and we all need support. Family and friends can be very supportive, but sometimes they're not, and that's where support groups come in. Remember what Dr. Vivek Murthy says in his book *Together*, that human beings are "hardwired for connection."

We need each other. It's in our nature to seek out connections. In fact, Murthy states, the lack of vital connections and especially isolation is one of the most serious causes of mental and physical decline and illnesses today. Don't go there. Don't let yourself isolate. You need others and they need you. And when you need some help, for heaven's sake, don't be timid about asking for it.

CHAPTER 5

"BEING MORTAL"

Thou, whose exterior semblance doeth belie
Thy soul's immensity.

~William Wordsworth

Medicine and What Matters in the End

Medicine and What Matters in the End is the subtitle for Dr. Atul Gawande's 2014 book *Being Mortal*. I promised I would recommend some books for you to read – put this one on the top of your list. I like it and so do dozens of reviewers. It was on the New York Times Bestseller List for over a year and selected as a best book of the year, which seems a bit strange for a book about dying. Gawande's book questions how the medical community approaches treating terminally ill patients. Writing in a very warm, personal manner with many case studies of people whom he has treated, he discusses, candidly, the challenges he has faced in his medical practice, as well as the challenges that the medical community faces as to the best ways to treat patients who are terminally ill.

I typically outline and reference important or interesting quotes in the back of the books I read for use in my own writing and classroom lectures, and I think I have more quotations referenced on the back pages of *Being Mortal* than any other book. If you have limited time for reading, I've included some of his most valuable quotes and ideas in this chapter; I've never written a chapter completely devoted to another author's book, but this one is certainly worth it.

Gawande tells the story of Felix Silverstone who, for five decades, was a national leader in geriatric medicine. Silverstone retired at age 82 in order to take care of his wife of more than 60 years. Following a time in the hospital for treatment of a heart attack, Felix was released back to his retirement home at Orchard Cove, a retirement facility in Massachusetts. Silverstone knew how to take care of himself physically but was worried about his emotional health, especially his periodic bouts of depression. What helped his emotional challenges, Gawande writes, was finding a purpose – a way to be of service to those around him. "He had been in Orchard Cove for only a few months before he was helping to steer a committee to improve the health care services there. He formed a journal-reading club for retired physicians. He even guided a young geriatrician through her first independent research study – a survey of residents' attitudes toward Do Not Resuscitate orders."

Gawande said that he doesn't like to promote the idea that endings are controllable. "No one ever really has control. Physics and biology and accidents ultimately have their way in our lives. But the point is that we are not helpless either. Courage is the strength to recognize both realities.... We have room to act, to shape our stories, though as time goes on it is within narrower and narrower confines. A few conclusions become clear when we treat the sick and the aged is the failure to recognize that they have priorities beyond merely being safe and living longer; that the chance to shape one's story is essential to sustain meaning in life; that we have the opportunity to refashion our institutions, our culture, and our conversations in ways that transform the possibilities for the last chapters of everyone's lives." That's very much the thesis of my book as well.

Purpose

Having a purpose is essential if you'd like to stay alive longer. The research is there. You will live longer if you have a reason to live (and you don't get hit by a car as you cross the street). Both are true. You will live longer if you have a reason to live – and there are no guarantees in life. You already know to look to the right when you're crossing a street in London; there are numerous signs on the sidewalk to remind Americans and others. You already know to be extra careful climbing ladders and descending staircases. Still, too many of us will visit the hospital with broken hips and other preventable injuries. Sadly, many more of us will die in the grip of depression, loneliness, and boredom. We may die earlier than we need to because, although we are cautious about crossing the street, we are careless about finding ways to connect with others and finding something valuable to live for.

You've developed the habit of watching out for yourself physically. What about the habit of cultivating your psychological or spiritual well-being? Apparently, Michelangelo had a purpose to live. He began the design of the dome of St. Peter's Basilica at age 71. Maybe that's not a fair comparison. Let's scale back a bit and look at writers, poets, and journalists who lived to be 100 years old or older. I counted close to 200 on Wikipedia's list of centenarians. Okay, you don't like to write? So, I went to Wikipedia's list of centenarians who were artists, painters, and sculptors – there were too many to count. Do actors and entertainers live long? Do your own research. It's good for your mental health to remain curious. You will live longer if you enjoy doing something interesting and worthwhile. According to research, a significant difference in death rates can be traced to an older person's success in finding a reason to live.

Yet, however well we prepare, aging happens. Gawande quoted Philip Roth from his novel, *Everyman*: "Old age is not a battle. Old age is a massacre." It's a massacre because however well we prepare, however well we fight the good fight, age will win. With luck and fastidiousness – eating well, exercising, keeping our blood pressure under control, getting medical help when we need it – people can often live a very long time.

However, Gawande reminds us that, over time, our daily living requirements will become more difficult for us to manage on our own and that a significant number of us will be unable to live independently. "As a result, most of us are unprepared for it. We rarely pay more than glancing attention to how we will live when we need help until it's too late to do much about it."

Essential Conversations

Besides having a purpose and being fastidious about your health is there anything else you should do to prepare? Yes – talk to people before it's too late to do much about it. Gawande illustrates such a conversation: "Susan Block and her father had the conversation that we all need to have when the chemotherapy stops working, when we start needing oxygen at home, when we face high-risk surgery, when the liver failure keeps progressing, when we become unable to dress ourselves. I've heard Swedish doctors call it a 'breakpoint discussion,' a series of conversations to sort out when they need to switch from fighting for time to fighting for the other things that people value – being with family or traveling or enjoying chocolate ice cream. Few people have these conversations, and there is good reason for anyone to become angry or overwhelmed. Managed poorly, the conversations can cost a person's trust. Managed well, they can take real time."

These conversations take "real time" because they are real conversations. It's so easy to skirt around unpleasant conversations. Difficult or not, these conversations end up being very valuable, especially for surviving family members. In her book, *Good to Go*, Jo Myers, writing about the surviving children of someone dying, suggests that "survivors have a better chance of a happy ending if parents make their wishes known, if they meet with family members as a tight-knit unit, if they have exit plans, and if they leave simple written instructions – even if the instructions are scribbled on a cocktail napkin."

"How are you?" people ask. "Just fine," we often reply, lying through our pearly whites. It's fine to say "fine." That's what we do when we meet someone at church, on the street, or in the store, when we don't have time to talk or don't want to get into what's really going on. I can't imagine anyone thinking that they are actually "just fine." Or if they are fine, it's because they have limited their scope. We are all dying. We are all missing someone. We are all facing choices and challenges. We all live in a world where people are suffering horribly. If we say we are fine, it's because we're not thinking about any of that, and sometimes that's okay. We can't constantly take the world on our shoulders or think about the unhappiness all around us. Still, there are times when it is important to have real conversations with those we care about.

Gawande reviewed a conversation between a father and daughter the evening before a delicate surgery. Dad and daughter talked about friends and family, avoiding the conversation that truly needed to happen. On her way home the daughter realized that they hadn't spoken about her father's wishes in the event that he didn't recover from surgery: "I realized, oh my God, I don't know what he really wants." Upon returning to the hospital, they resumed the vital discussion that the daughter needed to have. Dad reassured her that if he was able to survive the surgery and, later, if he would be able to eat chocolate ice cream and watch football, then he would be willing to go through the pain and do whatever was needed to stay alive. It's important to find the courage to have difficult conversations about the possibility of things getting worse and not better and what to do in those situations.

Years ago, I had a father and daughter as clients. They faced a difficult challenge. The daughter wanted to talk about the reality of her father's terminal illness – her dad didn't want to. "Please, Dad, this is something we need to discuss." To placate his daughter, the father was willing to see me together with his daughter. He wanted to enjoy the time he had left and was against talking about his end. "Do you want a memorial service, Dad? Who should I invite?" Dad sat quietly. "I really don't want to discuss this," he said. "I don't either, Dad, but I need to know what to do." She began to cry. "Dad, I need to know what to do!" Then her dad teared up, and replied, "I'm sorry, honey, whatever you want to do is fine." He reached over and took her hand and they cried together.

Letting Go

Letting go of people you love is incredibly hard to do. Gawande reports the statistic that in the U.S., 25% of Medicare spending goes to the 5% of people in the last year of their life, "and most of the money goes for care in their last couple of months that is of little apparent benefit." The statistics are similar in other countries. Letting go is hard to do. We hope for remission, for recovery – we want a miracle.

I don't think I could pull the plug. I don't even want to think about it. Kathe is much braver. She is very matter-of-fact about the end of her life. "Put me in a home with a gourmet chef," she says. "I'll be fine as long as I don't have to eat institutional food, and, for heaven's sake, don't keep me on a respirator or feeding tube. When it's my time, just let me go." We've had that conversation. We're in our early 70s, still relatively young, but we both know what the other wants in the event that one of us dies suddenly.

People who suffer from serious illnesses have other priorities besides simply staying alive. Among our main concerns as we age and face the end of our life is avoiding suffering, improving our relationships with our family and friends, being mentally alert, not being a burden on others, and finding peace that our life was meaningful. Gawande states that progress in technological medical care has failed to meet these needs, "and the cost of this failure is measured in far more than dollars. In 2008, the national Coping with Cancer project published a study showing that terminally ill cancer patients who were put on a mechanical ventilator, given electrical defibrillation or chest compression, or were admitted, near death, to intensive care, had a substantially worse quality of life in their last week that those who received no such interventions."

Most of us would like to die at home in our own beds surrounded by people we love. It is customary in many countries of the world to have older adults continue to live at home and be taken care of by family members. In some countries, not taking care of your elderly parents would be highly disrespectful and unthinkable. But for many reasons and for many people, trying to care for an elderly parent is inconvenient at best, and impossible at worst. So the first part of letting go may be the realization that as much as you might wish, you simply are unable to take care of an older person at home.

Sometimes, the person who is dying is the first to broach the awful conversation. The movie *Shadowlands* portrays the author C.S. Lewis' (played by Anthony Hopkins) three-year correspondence with an American woman, Joy Davidman. Joy (Debra Winger) visited Lewis at Oxford and they found themselves falling in love. Joy, always direct and outspoken, challenged Lewis to be more open to his emotions. Not long after their marriage, Joy found that she had cancer and didn't have long to live. On a pleasant holiday outing in the English countryside, Joy wanted to talk about her future. "Don't spoil it," Lewis said. "It doesn't spoil it," Joy said, "it makes it more real. I'm going to die and I want to be with you then too. The only way I can do that is if I'm able to talk to you about it now... The pain then is part of the happiness now. That's the deal." Lewis responded, "You've made me happy. I didn't know I could be so happy. You're the truest person I've ever known. I've just come up against a bit of experience. Experience is a brutal teacher, but you learn - my God you learn."

Lewis' comment reminded me of someone else who had a painful experience - the older client I've mentioned before, the one who lost his wife. In one of our sessions, he said to me, "The pain of that loss has softened my soul." I can't forget those words - they ring true. If we allow it, pain does soften our soul. It takes maturity and courage to let pain in and to let the pain do its work of creating more openness to the pain of others. Compassion (suffering with) is the fruit of not running away from one's own or another's suffering. It's easier to let go when you can let go of your own needs and find your heart of compassion for the one who is ready to leave.

Assisted Living (Continued)

In my last chapter, I discussed the concept of assisted living. Gawande devotes an entire chapter to explaining the psychological benefits of finding a suitable living environment for your later years. Gawande emphasizes the value of community. He blames his profession, the medical community, for placing too much emphasis on patients' physical health at the expense of their emotional health. "This simple but profound service – to grasp a fading man's need for everyday comforts, for companionship, for help achieving his modest aims – is the thing that is still so devastatingly lacking more than a century later."

A father and daughter decided on a compromise to assisted living. Dad would come home every Sunday through Tuesday. He could enjoy spending time with his family in familiar soundings. The rest of the week the daughter could focus on her own work and family. It worked for both of them. It's also true, however, that in time older adults are able to adjust. They make friends, they adjust to routines, and they find things to enjoy.

Gawande emphasizes that safety and physical health may be the most important considerations for older adults, but another important consideration is their mental and emotional well-being. Gawande ends this chapter with a reference to his grandfather's experience in India. "So this is the way it unfolds. In the absence of what people like my grandfather could count on – a vast extended family constantly on hand to let him make his own choices – our elderly are left with a controlled and supervised institutional existence, a medically designed answer to unfixable problems, a life designed to be safe but empty of anything they care about."

Still, sometimes it is possible to find good solutions. The second time Kathe's mom fell at home, Kathe knew that it was time for a change. Her brother had done some research and found a nursing home that seemed just right – a nice mix of safety and attentive staff as well as lots of enjoyable activities during the day. For her 94th birthday, we took Mom to her favorite restaurant. After the meal, Mom said that she was ready to go "home." We were surprised that the home she was talking about was her new living environment. She told us about the people she didn't like and the people she did like and, over time, she seemed to be quite content. I'll never forget her response to her daughter's question, "Mom, are you happy?" "Yes," she said, "I have no responsibilities!" Mom grew up on a farm in Indiana, moved to California for her husband's work, and spent her life raising her children. Now, at last, she had friends, a pleasant place to live, and "no responsibilities."

Another thing was interesting to Kathe and me. As Mom's life was drawing to a close and she was being visited by a hospice nurse, the nurse told us that although Mom was unable to respond, she could still hear us. When the nurse said that it was a matter of days, Kathe took her mom's hand, said that she loved her, that we would be fine, and that it would be okay for her to go home. Mom died the following morning.

A Novel Idea

Gawande tells the story of Bill Thomas, a doctor with an idea. He wanted to deal with the three plagues of nursing homes: boredom, loneliness, and helplessness. He decided that he needed to bring some life into the nursing home – literally. It wasn't easy and there was quite a bit of resistance from the staff who anticipated many more problems and a lot more work. Nevertheless, Thomas was determined. He brought in live plants, birds, parakeets, and birdcages, and, of course, dogs. "People who we had believed weren't able to speak started speaking," Thomas said. "People who had been completely withdrawn and non-ambulatory started coming to the nurses' station and saying, 'I'll take the dog for a walk.' All the parakeets were adopted and named by the residents. The lights turned back on in people's eyes. In a book he wrote about the experience, Thomas quoted from journals that the staff kept, and they described how irreplaceable the animals had become in the daily lives of residents, even ones with advanced dementia. Gawande cites a few staff journal entries:

> The inhabitants of Chase Memorial Nursing Home now included one hundred parakeets, four dogs, two cats, plus a colony of rabbits and a flock of laying hens. There were also hundreds of indoor plants and a thriving vegetable and flower garden. The home had on-site childcare for the staff and a new after-school program. Researchers studied the effects of this program over two years, comparing a variety of measures for Chase's residents with those of residents at another nursing home nearby. Their study found that the number of prescriptions required per resident fell to half that of the control group in the nursing home. Psychotropic drugs for agitation, like Haldol, decreased in particular. The total drug costs fell to just 3.8 percent of the comparison facility. Deaths fell 15 percent.

The Art of Dying

Dying used to be accompanied by a prescribed set of customs. Guides to *Ars Moriendi,* the art of dying, were extraordinarily popular; a medieval version published in Latin in 1415 was reprinted in more than a hundred editions across Europe. People believed death should be accepted stoically, without fear, self-pity, or hope for anything more than the forgiveness of God. Reaffirming one's faith, repenting one's sins, and letting go of one's worldly possessions and desires were crucial. These guides could provide families with prayers and questions for the dying in order to put them in the right frame of mind during their final hours. Last words came to hold a particular place of reverence.

At one point, Gawande was asked a very difficult question. Faced with the unlikelihood that a patient would survive complicated surgical procedures, he was asked, "Is she dying?" "I didn't know how to answer the question," Gawande writes. "I wasn't even sure what the word 'dying' meant anymore. In the past few decades, medical science has rendered obsolete centuries of experience, tradition, and language about our mortality and a new difficulty for mankind: how to die."

Reading that last sentence from Dr. Gawande reminded me of my first thoughts about the title of this book. My first title idea was *How to Die, A Travel Guide*. I'm not sure what gave me that idea. In the introduction to this book, I said that I wanted to be better prepared. Having written as much as I have, do I feel more prepared? I do feel more informed. I guess that may be good enough for now. Gawande reminds us that we only die once and we have no experience to draw on. We need doctors and nurses to be honest with us and have discussions with us about what they have seen and prepare us for what is to come.

I certainly agree with Gawande that doctors and nurses are likely to be the first to have those difficult conversations with patients who are dying and their family members. However, I have also seen a great number of recent publications in addition to *Being Mortal,* and this present work, that are addressing the topic of dying and being prepared. Gawande ends his book by writing a sobering message to the medical community. He warns that the concern for keeping someone physically alive may be at the expense of the emotional and relational needs of the person who is dying:

> People want to share memories, pass on wisdom and keepsakes, settle relationships, establish their legacy, make peace with God, and ensure that those who are left behind will be okay. They want to end their stories on their own terms. This role is, observers argue, among life's most important, for both the dying and those left behind. And if it is, the way we deny people this role, out of obtuseness and neglect, is cause for everlasting shame. Over and over, we in medicine inflict deep gouges at the end of people's lives and then stand oblivious to the harm done.

Gawande's caution is voiced throughout his book. He tells his readers, the medical community and all of us who are on our final journey, not to wait until we no longer have the ability or opportunity to end our story on our own terms. That doesn't mean, of course, that we have much of a say about what happens to us physically. Yet we do have a say in what to say. We can, as Gawande suggests, share memories, pass on wisdom and keepsakes, settle relationships, contribute to our legacy, and make peace with God; and, to reiterate what I have been saying throughout this book, it would be good to begin, or continue, to think about and talk about these things while we still can.

CHAPTER 6

———— • ————

FINDING GOODNESS, BEAUTY, AND GRATITUDE ON THE JOURNEY

Where beauty has no ebb, decay no flood,
But joy is wisdom, Time an endless song.
~ From *Land of Hearts Desire* by William Butler Yeats

Goodness, beauty, and gratitude – these qualities go together, don't they? – thank God. Life is hard. It takes a toll on all of us. For some, life is unimaginably hard. Nevertheless, in the midst of ugliness and brutality, there are still golden moments of goodness, tenderness, and beauty. Listen to what Victkor Frankl had to say about one freezing morning in a Nazi concentration camp:

> In camp, too, a man might draw attention of a comrade working next to him to a nice view of the setting sun shining through the tall trees of the Bavarian woods. . . . Standing outside we saw sinister clouds glowing in the west and the whole sky alive with clouds of ever-changing shapes and colors, from steel blue to blood red. The desolate gray mud huts provided a sharp contrast while the puddles on the muddy ground reflected the glowing sky. Then, after minutes of moving silence, one prisoner said to another, "How beautiful the world could be!"

I think for many of us, being grateful may become harder as we get older. We're falling apart. We don't look like we used to, we don't move around as easily, we don't heal as quickly, and our memory fails us at times. What is there to be grateful for?

What is there to be grateful for? – a lot; but it may require regular transfusions of goodness and beauty to find that place of gratitude within. The key to experiencing beauty is to look for it. In fact, the key to not becoming depressed and disillusioned about life, especially as we get older, is to focus attention on looking for the goodness and beauty around us. If you look for it, you will see it.

What is meant by the word goodness? The two most common uses of the word "goodness" are, first, the state of being good or virtuous, and second, the nutritious, flavorful, or beneficial part of something. Do you see the connection? There is something wonderfully satisfying and nutritious about goodness. Doing good or observing someone doing good touches us in a particularly satisfying way, a way that reflects "how beautiful the world could be." The internet, despite all of its distractions and meanness, is one place to find acts of kindness, love, and goodness. Apparently, people enjoy posting illustrations of people being kind and thoughtful to others. A major news story aired on August 10th, 2022 depicting a young little leaguer who had been hit in the head by a fastball. He was wearing a helmet so the ball knocked him to the ground and stung but didn't seriously injure him. The pitcher was terribly shaken up by what happened and stood frozen on the mound when the young batter approached him and gave him a consoling hug. That scene of forgiveness and generous kindness was truly beautiful.

My wife is especially fond of clips of unlikely animal pals cuddling with each other. If you believe in the concept of the human spirit, then you can believe that goodness nurtures one's spirit. Jack Canfield and Mark Victor Hansen have already figured that out and created that delightful series, *Chicken Soup for the Soul.*

Beauty

When you take time to look for the good, be grateful that you're also more apt to see the beauty around you. I think this is what the Irish poet John O' Donohue was saying in his book *Beauty*: "When we walk on the earth with reverence, beauty will decide to trust us. The rushed heart and the arrogant mind lack the gentleness and patience to enter that embrace. Beauty is mysterious, a slow presence who waits for the ready expectant heart." Indeed, for many of us, one of the blessings of being older is having more time, being less hurried and harried, and being more available for the embrace of beauty.

In the film *The Horse Whisperer*, Annie (Kristin Scott Thomas) says to Tom (Robert Redford), about his 85-year-old mother: "I envy your mother. It must be great to be her age and to be at the point in life where you have no more guesswork. . . no more responsible decisions to make and anyway, it doesn't matter because all the worries and all the wrong turns that you made are so valuable and as cherished as the things you did right. Must be such a relief, must be such peace in that."

I've noticed a remarkable change in myself since I retired a couple of years ago. I'm much less impatient, more at peace. I was trying to explain the feeling to my wife recently. She replied, "You're less compressed." As usual, she was exactly right. Like most of us, I grew up with lots of responsibilities. I had homework, chores, sports, part-time work, and helping my dad with yard work on Saturdays. After a while, it seems that one's body and mind take on the habit of being busy – becoming compressed. So, I wondered what it would feel like when I retired and no longer averaged seeing around forty clients a week and teaching one or two graduate classes. It turns out, I love it. Many retired folks continue to stay busy. So do I, but I'm no longer compressed. Unlike my former life, when I always felt rushed and burdened, I no longer mind waiting in line – I take a book to the DMV. I used to be incensed when someone cut me off on the freeway or darted around me because I wasn't driving fast enough. Now I find myself simply being grateful that I'm not that person. I don't have to hurry anywhere. Sitting in traffic still bothers me though – I'm no saint.

I like the idea of taking time to step out of the "blur of busyness," to notice the trees dancing in the wind or seeing shapes in the clouds. I recall a time of pruning roses in my garden. It was twilight on a warm spring evening and I was listening to a beautiful aria on the radio (remember those?). I think one sign that we're in the presence of beauty is that we can't move; and so, I was arrested. The spring air and lovely aria held me captive. I sat down on a nearby bench and breathed in the golden moment, what might be called a peak experience. Abraham Maslow wrote about peak experiences as an indescribable time of feeling arrested, not wanting to be anywhere else, of experiencing a moment of transcendence, sometimes euphoria, perhaps realizing something of vital importance. You can't orchestrate peak experiences, but you can learn to ready your heart for when they arrive. You can learn to take time to sit still and be open to the breaking forth of something sublime, whether around you or within you.

In his 2006 book *Integral Spirituality*, Ken Wilber had fun with Maslow's idea of a peak experience. He said that as you mature in your spiritual awareness, you might be granted a "peek" experience in which you can see further into the possibilities of your own spiritual development. For Wilber, growth in your spirituality occurs as you open your heart to what is true, what is good, and what is beautiful. You are honoring spirit, according to Wilber, when you allow beauty to enter your life. Wilber echoes the writings of O'Donohue. You see the beauty around you when you slow down, occasionally stepping out of the blur - when you look for it, when you ready your heart and are watchful for a moment where you can be overtaken by beauty.

I hadn't "readied" my heart as I was racing through the Tate Gallery in London, trying to see as much as I could in the hour that I had available. I turned a corner of the gallery and in front of me was Joseph Mallord William Turner's painting, "Norham Castle, Sunrise." I was arrested by its beauty. Turner perfectly added enough of a location in light blue in order to highlight the radiant light emanating from, seemingly, behind the canvas itself. For me, this was not only an experience of beauty, but of transcendent spirituality. I stared it for a long time and had to tear myself away. It was, and remains, a peak experience for me.

For Wilber, there are three primary stages of spiritual/emotional development which he describes in *Integral Spirituality,* and the "peek" experience is one that occurs in higher levels of spiritual/emotional growth. He terms the first major life stage "preconventional." This is an egocentric stage where toddlers or young children feel that the world revolves around them and haven't yet learned to behave according to society's conventions. Stage two is the "conventional" stage of morals. Wilber writes, "This stage is also called ethnocentric, in that it centers on the child's particular family, group, tribe, clan, or nation, and it therefore tends to exclude those not of one's group." In the next major stage of moral development, the "postconventional" stage, "the individual's identity expands once again, this time to include a care and concern for all peoples, regardless of race, color, sex, or creed, which is why this stage is also called worldcentric. Thus, moral development tends to move from 'me' (egocentric) to 'us' (ethnocentric) to 'all of us' (worldcentric) – a good example of the unfolding stages of consciousness." So, for Wilber, a peak experience can also be a "peek" experience, where we are suddenly able to view, and even visit, higher levels of consciousness and of moral development. This may happen as a mountaintop experience or a profound religious experience. The ineffable moment of connection expands our awareness of the vastness of the universe and our small but potentially powerful place in it. This higher level of consciousness may also occur over time as we attend to our own spiritual disciplines. John Keats said it well: "I feel more and more every day, as my imagination strengthens, that I do not live in this world alone but in a thousand worlds."

This may be the reason that older people seem to enjoy going to church more than younger people. I thought when I was younger that there are more older people in church because now that they're old, they need to believe that they are going to heaven. Now I don't think that's the reason - many people are actually less afraid of death when they're older. I think the reason is that they have not only grown emotionally and intellectually, but they have also grown spiritually. There is more of them available to experience their experiences: to "feel more and more every day, as [their] imagination strengthens...." Keats was reminding us that, while we live in the "finite," the "infinite" lives within us. As we mature, we have the capability to see more deeply into the infinite. We are more prepared to *peek* into eternal truths which are ready to reveal to us what is truly valuable. We are increasingly aware of the value of all human beings instead of staying stuck in an ethnocentric stage of "me, us four, and no more."

Gratitude

Yes, it is difficult to be grateful at times. For some, it is difficult all the time. A common theme in the religions of the world is to practice gratitude. For people recovering from addictions, practicing gratitude helps keep them alive. A client of mine, a former alcoholic who had been sober for many years, told me that when he begins to feel resentful and burdened by life, he knows that it's time to visit people in prison. He reminds himself to be grateful that he is no longer locked up in the prison of his addiction. I know this may be a stretch for many people, but if you can imagine that the experience of being alive is a type of classroom experience, then it's possible to be grateful, even for the hard lessons.

According to an August 2017 article in *Lifeskills* of South Florida, Robert Emmons, a professor of psychology at the University of California, Davis, states, "The practice of gratitude can have dramatic and lasting effects in a person's life." His study of gratitude states that a sense of gratitude gives many personal benefits. These benefits range from the physical to the psychological and even to the social and the relational.

Physical
- Reduced sensing of aches and pains
- Stronger immune systems
- Lower blood pressure

- Increased interest in exercise and taking care of health
- Better, more restful sleep

Psychological
- Increased levels of positive emotions
- Increased alertness, aliveness, and awareness
- Increased sense of joy and pleasure
- Increased feelings of worthiness, optimism, and happiness

Social
- Increased desire to be helpful, generous, and compassionate
- Increased feelings of forgiveness
- Increased interest in being outgoing
- Reduced feelings of loneliness and isolation

The article concludes, "Practicing gratitude not only affects the thoughts and behaviors of those suffering from addiction or 'dual diagnosis' in recovery [mental illness combined with substance abuse], but it also has profound implications on the way we interact with the world around us. Gratitude allows an individual to celebrate the present and be an active participant in life."

Mindfulness

Many of us have only a vague understanding of the word "meditation." We may remember when the Beatles spent time learning to meditate with their guru Maharishi Mahesh Yogi, who popularized the discipline of transcendental meditation as a mode of spiritual development. The problem with the word "meditation," though, is that it is frequently associated with Eastern religious practices prioritizing stillness that are less appealing to busy Westerners. Another problem with the word is that it is not clearly understood – what exactly is the goal of meditation? Americans like goals.

If we change the term "meditation" to the more scientific-sounding term "mindfulness," the problem is solved. Divorce mindfulness from associations with Eastern religion and now it's easier and more acceptable to discuss the value of "mindfulness training" (it sounds more scientific, and Americans like science). The term "mindfulness" appeared around 1970 when Jon Kabat-Zinn, who after having studied meditation techniques, developed a program called Mindfulness-Based Stress Reduction (MBSR) to treat chronic pain. Since research has affirmed that practicing mindfulness is a successful approach to pain management as well as stress management, the term has become more acceptable and popular.

Mindfulness training has now entered mainstream science and medicine and has become a central part of Mindfulness-Based Cognitive Therapy, Dialectical Behavior Therapy, and dozens of books and internet instructions on sites like YouTube. I have a few of these books in my library including *The Mindful Brain*, *The Mindful Therapist*, *Mindful Therapy*, and others. These have become valuable sources of insight into effective therapy for stress management and relaxation training. Having frequently recommended mindfulness training to my clients, I find the easiest exercise to do is in your car. Wait 60 seconds after arriving at your destination before reaching for the car door. This is a good way to practice mindful meditation and stepping out of the "blur." While you're sitting, pray, practice gratitude, do nothing, just sit quietly. Do the same thing when you get back into your car – wait another 60 seconds before starting the ignition.

Why Mindfulness?

What is the value of mindfulness training? I'll quote from the periodical *Psychology Today*:

> Mindfulness encompasses two key ingredients: awareness and acceptance. Awareness is the knowledge and ability to focus attention on one's inner processes and experiences, such as the experience of the present moment. Acceptance is the

ability to observe and accept – rather than judge or avoid – those streams of thought. The goal of mindfulness is to cultivate perspective on one's consciousness and identity that can bring greater peace mentally and relationally. Mindfulness may also be used in mindfulness-based therapies, to address stress, anxiety, or pain, and simply to become more relaxed.

This chapter is about beauty, goodness, and gratitude. I think it is also about being more mindful, which includes learning to pay closer attention to the things that matter. Being mindful is the art of enjoying being alive.

"The Radiance of the Good Makes Beauty Real"

I quoted the poet John O'Donohue above. He also wrote that "when you take the time to travel with reverence, a richer life unfolds before you. Moments of beauty begin to braid your day." In my mind, walking with reverence is walking expectantly, mindfully, attentive to the possibility that beauty will find you. O'Donoghue also connects goodness to beauty: "The life-journey can be a union with the Beautiful – the radiance of the Good makes beauty real."

What could he possibly mean that "the radiance of the Good makes beauty real?" I think he understands that observing true goodness is a beautiful experience. As I walked out of a worship service recently, I found three dads holding and quieting their infants. I wish I had my phone or camera. What a beautiful sight – a mixture of love and goodness – the love of a father and the goodness to comfort an infant while giving others the space, undistracted, to enjoy the service. Seeing someone giving an older person his seat, watching someone holding the door for a mom with a stroller – goodness is visible every day – and it is beautiful.

I said at the beginning of this chapter that goodness, beauty, and gratitude go together. Why do you think that is? It may be because they are qualities of Spirit. Recall my contention earlier that a human being is a mixture of the dirt of the earth and the breath of God, and the soul is the connection between. The soul is the place of wrestling and searching. We wrestle with the pull of the earth on the one hand – with our biology, our appetites, and our fears. We wrestle on the other hand with the pull of our spirit, with what we know is of infinite value. We search for meaning and balance – balance between necessity and possibility, and between the finite and the infinite. When we fall out of balance, beauty and goodness help to bring us back. Gratitude keeps us on the right road, on our journey home. I love this quote from Elisabeth Kubler-Ross: "People are like stained glass windows. They sparkle and shine when the sun is out, but when the darkness sets in, their true beauty is revealed only if there is a light from within."

Light from within is an interesting concept. I'm reminded of the Quaker idea of "inner light." In the mid-17th century, George Fox met with his "society of friends" and spoke of an inner light or inward light, that portion of God's spirit that is given to every human being for direction and illumination. Fox insisted that "inner light" isn't simply a mystical concept, but also the impulse to do good in the world. In this Fox confirms the idea that true spiritual illumination will necessarily translate into bringing good into being.

George Harrison wrote a song titled "The Inner Light" in which he describes the fruit of his experience with transcendental meditation – the ability to see the world (as William Blake might have said) by looking within. Apparently, Morgan Gendel, the freelance writer who wrote the award-winning 125th episode of *Star Trek: The Next Generation*, titled "The Inner Light," was inspired by the George Harrison song. One wonders if this idea of inner light might be an archetype of spiritual awareness. If so, like all archetypes, it seems to exist across time and place, showing up in art, literature, music, and religious thought. But it shows up in other places as well.

What is Truly Beautiful?

One answer to that question is, "It depends." I couldn't simply walk by Turner's painting. It arrested me, stopped me in my tracks, spoke to me. My guess is that it hasn't had the same effect on everyone. Does true beauty manifest itself in ways that touch all of us? What is the truly beautiful? Why hang this painting in an art museum and not another one? The art historian Robert McIntosh says, "Art should speak for itself. That's why when you go to a gallery, you stare at different pieces and let them speak to you. That is the true beauty of art, the potential to communicate without using any words." So, another answer to the question of what is truly beautiful may be that the experience is personally meaningful. Can there be experiences of beauty that are meaningful to all of us? That's worth thinking about.

It may be that what is truly beautiful has a timeless quality. I'm thinking about Michelangelo's Pietas, for example – he carved two, one at 23 years of age and the other in his seventies (images of both are easily found on the internet). The first Pieta in St. Peter's Basilica is probably the more famous. It shows the confidence of the young Michelangelo in carving a lifelike figure of the mother of Christ holding her dead son. People who have known loss, profound loss, can easily relate to Mary's grief.

One might not call Michelangelo's second Pieta beautiful in the customary sense of the word. Its beauty is resident in the emotion evident in the figures, especially the hooded man. Some art critics see Michelangelo himself depicted in that figure. Apparently, he was so frustrated with having to carve on the uncooperative marble, combined with his failing strength, that he smashed a portion of the statue with a hammer and stormed out, leaving the work unfinished. Michelangelo intended the statue for his own tomb but abandoned the idea and never returned to his second masterpiece. What seems to be timeless and gripping about this work is that it vividly portrays the agony of life – the agony of living daily within the paradox of the excruciating beauty in the world, on the one hand, against the profound and universal suffering on the other. Is his work beautiful? It does meet the criteria of arresting, illuminating, and transcendent.

Perhaps, for some, beauty can be seen as a father holding his newborn; for others, the carpet of a forest glade illuminated by streams of light; for others, a sunset in Polynesia. Beauty may be that which takes us to a different place inside, a place we haven't visited or haven't visited enough. When you think about your life, the times when you have experienced true beauty, what comes to your mind? It would be good to reflect on those experiences again and again. Spend time remembering those experiences, for they will nourish your soul. Carson, the butler in the popular television series *Downton Abbey* said: "The business of life is the acquisition of memories. In the end, that's all there is."

Michelangelo's final Pieta is housed in the Museo dell 'Opera del Duomo in Florence. On the wall behind you, as you view the statue, is the sonnet "Old Age," by poet Henry Wadsworth Longfellow. One side is in Italian and the other in English. The sonnet reads:

> The course of my long life hath reached at last,
> In fragile bark o'er a tempestuous sea,
> The common harbor, where must rendered be
> Account of all the actions of the past.
> The impassioned phantasy, that, vague and vast,
> Made art an idol and a king to me,
> Was an illusion, and but vanity
> Were the desires that lured me and harassed.
> The dreams of love, that were so sweet of yore,
> What are they now, when two deaths may be mine, –
> One sure, and one forecasting its alarms?
> Painting and sculpture satisfy no more
> The soul now turning to the Love Divine,
> That oped, to embrace us, on the cross its arms.

It seems that Longfellow came to the same conclusion as did Solomon in the Bible – one must not make a god of one's possessions, creations, or contributions. It is all "vanity." There will come a time when they "satisfy no more." What has lasting beauty and value is "turning to the Love Divine." Maybe Michelangelo knew this early in his life but came to a more profound and personal appreciation as his journey was nearing its end, and thus, the museum chose to celebrate his last Pieta with this sonnet.

T.S. Eliot wrote, "Poetry, like music, should communicate before it is understood." You don't have to understand a poem, a piece of music or a work of art to be engaged by its beauty. As you look deeper into that particular work that engages you, you see something of the eternal speaking to you, reminding you to pay attention, reminding you of what is important in life. In looking at what is beautiful we learn to see what is good. In this way, the experience of beauty is a doorway to the journey beyond.

CHAPTER 7

———————— ● ————————

CREATIVITY AND COMMUNITY

Unwillingness to fully participate in being leaves a hole in the world the size of your soul in the cultural landscape.

~Jordan Peterson

Sitting at a table with six other oldies, I thought to myself, "Thank goodness." Thank goodness for this artists' association and our monthly meetings for dinner and a painting demonstration. This evening's demonstration was given by an artist who specializes in still-life paintings of vases of flowers, as well as portraits. She stood in front of a camera that projected her careful brush strokes on a screen for all 60 of us to see. And most of the 60 of us were well over 60. In fact, at my table sat a woman born in Europe in 1938 who somehow managed to survive the world wars. Sitting next to her was a woman born in 1935 in the U.S. who remembers rationing and victory gardens. They both enjoy doing watercolors. The gentleman on my right painted in oils and acrylics in addition to doing occasional sculptures. The interesting thing about this gathering was that we were all still alive – very much alive.

Many of us at the dinner had been painting for decades, but we all knew that there was still more to learn. The wonderful thing about a creative project is that, often, the project is creating you. I was struck by the curiosity and liveliness of the group. Liveliness is the right word. The people at my table were enthusiastic about what they were doing, eager to share with each other, eager to learn, and eager to try out new ideas. In addition to our creative interests, all of us had stories to tell.

Many of the stories were of family, and especially of grandchildren. Many of the stories were about visits to the doctor or the hospital and our ongoing physical challenges. Many of the stories found us roaring with laughter. The wonderful thing about these tablemates was the mutual enjoyment of community and communion.

This book is about your final journey and how to prepare for your eventual death. Yet who wants to die just because there's nothing to keep you alive? Sadly, some people may die sooner rather than later because of sheer boredom, loneliness, or both. A reviewer of Dr. Vivek Murthy's book *Together* states: "An invisible crisis plagues America today. It's responsible for more sickness, suffering, and death, than almost anything else. It is loneliness. It is often underneath addictions, suicide and even obesity.... The science is clear - the most powerful force to heal is love and connection. Community is medicine."

All of us have probably had the experience of being lonely in a room full of people who know us and love us. How can that be? The answer to that question is both simple and complicated. The simple answer is that we, ourselves, may not be fully present. Even though we are surrounded by lovely people, we may not be fully open to them because we haven't been fully open to ourselves. We haven't yet accessed or affirmed the riches that lay within - our own value - our ability to touch the hearts of others. So, we sit uncomfortably with the feeling that we have very little to offer. Sadly, it's hard to feel interesting when it doesn't feel like there's anything interesting inside.

Knowing Your Value

The key question isn't "What fosters creativity?" But it is why, in God's name, isn't everyone creative? Where was the human potential lost? How was it crippled? I think therefore a good question might be not why do people create? But why do people not create or innovate? We have got to abandon that sense of amazement in the face of creativity, as if it were a miracle if anybody created anything.

~Abraham Maslow

The answer to Maslow's question, of course, is that too many people are preoccupied with self-doubt. There was a time when we were taught not to call attention to ourselves. We were taught not to be a showoff or think that we were better than others. That's good advice when it's balanced with encouragement to develop healthy self-worth. Being modest about oneself is a virtue – when it doesn't interfere with self-worth. I don't know, maybe the pendulum has swung too far. Listen to the song "Participation Award" on YouTube. The humorous idea behind the song is that everyone should be able to be a winner and get a trophy, even for just showing up. However, giving out unearned trophies isn't the way to develop healthy self-worth. Self-worth isn't about being good at something or better than someone else. Self-worth is about character. Have you made some good choices in your life? Have you chosen, at times, to forgive, to reach out, to be kind? These are qualities of character. Be happy that you've been that person. You don't have to be good at doing something. You simply need to be good at being a good you.

If you'd like to be more creative, expand the idea of creativity to having fun. Remember back to the days when we were taught to fingerpaint? It was fun. You really couldn't get it wrong. One of my friends creates greeting cards using the same techniques of cutting and pasting that we learned in kindergarten (she's progressed significantly in her craft). Why does she do it? Because it's fun. Why am I taking time to encourage you to find a way to be creative? Because you're still alive, and being creative will help you to stay alive. Recall that when you create something, that something is creating you. The "energy out" from the creative *doing* is multiplied by the "energy in" from *being* creative. The word "recreation" is a good word to describe the inward flow of joyful enthusiasm arising from a creative project that you love doing. It doesn't especially matter what that project is as long as you're having fun doing it.

Creativity isn't limited to *making* something. You can be creative by *doing* something. It won't be hard to find a need in your community, place of worship, neighborhood, or school. Of course, there are plenty of opportunities for volunteer work. In addition, there are many groups for doing fun activities with others. You name it, and there's a group for it: hiking, biking, sailing, cold-water swimming, art guilds, quilting, sewing, mahjong, book clubs, bowling leagues, and more. I could fill a chapter or two. I recently joined a group of retired folks who enjoy playing pickleball. I'd never heard of pickleball until someone said to me, "You're not really retired unless you play pickleball." So, I joined. I don't need to say much more about groups for fun and recreation. Anyone can start one and anyone can lead one. Most people already know about the Meetup website, which includes information on various groups in your area as well as instructions on how to start a group. The important thing is to appreciate that joining is creating. You're creating a place to *be* with others and perhaps a place to *do* things with others. Creativity and connection will keep you alive longer. It will also help you to want to stay alive. Here's why…

Connection is Medicine

In 2020 I wrote the book *Growing Groups* for a graduate class I teach at Pepperdine University. The textbook instructs students on how to develop and lead various types of groups. Here's an excerpt from my book.

> In his 2008 book *Outliers*, Malcolm Gladwell wrote about the Mystery of Roseto, Pennsylvania. The mystery was why, between 1954 and 1961, Roseto had nearly no heart attacks among the otherwise high-risk group of men 55 to 65. In 1961, Dr. Stewart Wolf, the head of medicine at the University of Oklahoma, studied what has now become known as the "Roseto Effect." The doctor wondered why deaths from heart disease were so low. The men of this Italian American community ate poorly, drank wine in excess, smoked, and worked in dangerous conditions in a slate mine, just like they did in Italy. So, what was the reason? The reason, Dr. Wolf wrote in a 1963 paper on the Roseto effect, was community. Just as they did in Italy, the

newly arrived Italian immigrants, mainly from the same village in Roseto, brought with them their extended families and their culture of connection. Connection, and community, it turns out, play a vital role in mental and physical well-being. The "mystery" isn't a mystery. The community shared the common values of a close-knit social structure, a structure with little competition for status, a willingness to help each other in times of need, and a value on people not because of what they possessed or achieved but because they belonged. The best antidote for the stresses of normal living, financial worries, envy, and competition to get ahead, is knowing that you are not alone. Other people are there to help when you need them. Love is good for your health. When a person feels valued, supported, connected, that person is more likely to survive.

The three psychiatrists who wrote *A General Theory of Love* (2001), Dr. Thomas Lewis, Dr. Fari Amini, and Dr. Richard Lannon, powerfully confirm that connection is medicine. They write, "Medicine lost sight of this truth: attachment is physiology. Good physicians have always known that the relationship heals." In *Growing Groups,* I wrote, "We have inherited the good news and the bad news of living in a modern Western culture. We know all about the good news. The bad news is that we are suffering from some of the consequences of the good news. As you might expect, as the village of Roseto, Pennsylvania 'progressed' into the 20th and 21st century, so did the death rate from heart disease."

A competitive society is a good thing when it doesn't drive us into early graves. This is the problem that Dr. Murthy tackles in *Together*. A serious problem with living in a competitive society is social isolation, often caused by feelings of inadequacy. Loneliness, according to Murthy and much of the medical community, is making us sick. "We are wired for connection," Murthy says. The lack of connection increases our stress hormones which results in an increase in our vulnerability to physical and emotional illness. When people are lonely, it's tempting for them to think that there may be something wrong with them. Perhaps, they imagine, "I'm not very interesting, or friendly enough, or have anything of value to contribute." Murthy's research suggests that this self-perception may create a vicious cycle of depression and withdrawal, a self-perpetuating, self-fulfilling prophecy leading to increased loneliness. Lonely people look for comfort. When they withdraw from people for self-protection out of fear of judgment or rejection, they may turn to self-harming behaviors. Research shows a direct connection between loneliness and isolation with addictive behaviors such as increased alcohol consumption, obesity, diabetes, and other physical illnesses. As I wrote in *Growing Groups*, "We are all so much together, but we are all dying of loneliness."

Murthy's statement that there is an epidemic of loneliness in this country is quite ironic in this "communication age." Clearly, it's the *type* of communication that's the problem. It's fun to stay in touch with family and friends online but is that real connection? Look up the hormonal effects of hugging. You've heard that the chemical oxytocin has been called the "love hormone" because it surges through lovers when they embrace. But it's also called the "snuggle hormone" because a genuine hug will have similar effects on any two people. How wonderful it would be if more people visited nursing or retirement homes with the sole purpose of giving out hugs. I know a retired person whose sole responsibility three days a week is to show up at the newborn nursery section of a local hospital to hold and rock infants. What a great way to spend an afternoon.

The Covid-19 pandemic hit us hard. A 2020 United Nations report on the social impact of Covid stated that among the lethal effects was an increase in stress-related illnesses due to chronic anxiety and social isolation. Everyone has felt the effects. The virus infected our social and political institutions as well. Without the comforting connections of hugs and handshakes, it's easier to be irritable, resentful, self-protective, and polarized. Maybe I'm wrong, but during Covid, I seemed to notice more drivers speeding and being reckless and inconsiderate as if they were taking out their anger and frustrations on the road. More than ever, we need the physical and psychological benefits of connection. We will all die. Hopefully we won't die alone and unloved.

Vulnerability and Trust

When M. Scott Peck published *A Different Drum* in 1987, he outlined the requirements to form an authentic community. What is an "authentic" community? In any gathering of people, Peck calls the first stage of community development "pseudo community." By this he means the typical polite small talk that characterizes most meetings of service organizations, social clubs, places of worship and so forth. Of course there's nothing wrong with this common social convention of getting acquainted or catching up with friends, but this is not what Peck thinks of as a true community.

It isn't typical for people to share deep hurts or vulnerable confessions at a social gathering. In fact, much of the time it wouldn't be appropriate to burden or annoy people with unsolicited intimate information. That type of sharing is saved for close friends, family, or small groups. Even in those contexts, however, it's difficult, having developed the habit of being self-protective, to trust that it's okay to share vulnerable information. The largest hurdle to overcome in transitioning out of pseudo community is the challenge of vulnerability and trust.

Most people aren't very good listeners. If you need proof, try talking about politics, the pandemic, religion, or any other controversial topic you can think of. You will likely spark a debate. There's certainly nothing wrong with a friendly debate, as long as it's friendly, or at least civil. But debating isn't listening. Good listening skills require practice, and bringing up an uncomfortable topic often results in someone giving advice, correcting perceptions, and trying to convert the other to a different way of thinking or believing. How vulnerable can you be when faced with these kinds of responses?

Peck calls the second stage of community development "chaos." This occurs in groups when someone makes an effort to be real, to be vulnerable, to share uncomfortable emotions, and they're met with the negative responses I cited above. This kind of confusion and potential conflict negates the opportunity to compassionately listen and care for another's story. Of course this is why, lacking trust in the benefits of sharing, people are typically reluctant to be open and vulnerable.

Stage three in community development is when friends, family members, or people in a small group suspend their need to fix, heal, convert, or correct, and simply listen. Peck calls this stage "emptiness." This is surprisingly difficult when you care about someone and want desperately to help. The best help you can often give is to show compassion (from the Latin to "suffer with").

You suspend your agenda to "help" and are simply present with careful and compassionate listening. In the language of therapy, this is called "attunement." This quality of compassion and the ability to come alongside someone who is hurting constitutes true or "authentic" community. Vulnerability occurs in the presence of trust. As trust grows so does the quality of sharing that is transformative. Healing, connection, and a greater capacity to love are the results.

Attunement

In his 1951 publication, *Client-Centered Therapy*, the psychologist Carl Rogers moved the field of psychotherapy into a revolutionary new direction from traditional forms of therapy. In fact, a survey was conducted in 1982 asking 422 U.S. and Canadian psychologists whom they considered to be the most influential psychotherapist in modern history. The answer was Carl Rogers. Rogers' approach was radical in his insistence on offering a *quality of connection* between client and therapist. Since the early days of Freud, psychology followed the medical model of the doctor-patient relationship. The doctor diagnosed the patient's symptoms and proscribed a cure. This was usually done through providing analysis and insight. It was often an effective way to help patients with their mental or emotional problems. However, Rogers wanted to approach helping people differently.

Rogers noticed that many people suffered because they isolated themselves from others, tied up in what Rogers termed "conditions of worth" (I'm okay if..., I'm okay when...). If the therapist offered "unconditional positive regard," "empathic listening," and "genuine-ness," Rogers' observed, the client's symptoms improved. In Rogers' early career, he had worked with returning WWII veterans. These were individuals unaccustomed to discussing their emotions. But the warmth and caring Rogers provided broke through the vulnerability barrier of the veterans and they were able to find the courage to discuss the trau-mas they had experienced in battle. His successes were documented in a 1946 paper, "Counseling with Returned Servicemen." Rogers con-cluded that a "non-directive" method of therapy was more effective than the directive approach used in the traditional medical model. Over time, it was obvious that this client-centered approach would be effective in many other contexts as well. So, the title "client-centered" was changed to "person-centered" therapy.

The key to the effectiveness of this approach is the quality of the connection between the client and therapist. The term used for this quality of connection in psychology is "attunement." The psychiatrist Dan Siegel describes the benefits of attunement as the experience of "feeling felt." You know that feeling. When you're talking to someone who is genuinely interested and caring, and there seems to be an in-visible shared energy field of understanding at a deeply human level, you are experiencing "attunement," that ineffable quality of human connection. In that place, you feel known and valued. It is a rich source of energy that can be healing and transformative. When you find that feeling in a group of people, you are experiencing authentic commu-nity.

Over many years of research and practice, therapists now know that Rogers was right. The quality of attunement between therapist and cli-ent is curative and transformative. The authors of *A General Theory of Love* have this to say about attunement:

If a listener quiets his neocortical chatter and allows limbic sensing to range free, melodies begin to penetrate the static of anonymity. Individual tales of reactions, hopes, expectations, and dreams resolve into themes…. As the listener's resonance grows, he will catch sight of what the other sees inside that personal world, start to sense what it feels like to live there.

Here, the authors are encouraging therapists to follow Rogers' advice and listen deeply into what the client is saying. The same possibility for profound communion is available to anyone who is willing to set aside his or her "neocortical chatter," including thoughts, advice, or direction, and simply allow themselves to become porous to the inner world of another.

Have you had that experience? Do you have a friend or life partner who is practiced at being porous, who is able to combine quality listening with quality caring? If so, you have been blessed. You know how it feels to *feel felt*. Research shows an experience like this can keep you alive longer, or, at least, increase the quality of your life. It would be good if you could be a person who can offer that depth of caring to another. This is the "authentic community" that M. Scott Peck advocated for.

Creativity

What do you think of when you read the word "creativity?" Is it creating a song, a poem, or a painting? Those things are clearly creative. Do you ever think about creating a day, your day, a day that you can feel good about? That's also creative. What would that day look like? What would it feel like? Are you too discouraged and tired of life to be able to imagine giving yourself a creative kind of a day? Maybe you could give it to someone else. What would that take? It would take being creative.

Creativity is a spiritual exercise. What does that mean? Genesis, the first book of the Old Testament, announces God's will for His creation. (I could just as easily use the term, "Her creation.") God's will for creation, for you and me, is to be a co-creator with God – to bring life and order into the world. There are countless ways to do that.

Creating Community

Remember what Dr. Vivek Murthy told us, that we are hard-wired for connection. Maybe even the people who are tired of people and who crave a solitary life are looking for connection – they may be craving more connection with themselves, or with nature, or with God. Kathe and I watched the television series *Homestead Rescue*. Kathe was enthralled by the ingenious ways people find to live off the grid. I was curious about what motivates them. Again and again, what seems to motivate people is independence – the ability to depend solely on themselves, on their own ingenuity and creativity. The show is all about creativity. In addition, the show demonstrates how difficult it is to exist without needing help from time to time. So sometimes the call for help goes out to the homestead rescuers and sometimes to extended family or neighboring friends. It is very hard to survive alone.

When I think of solitude, John Muir and Henry David Thoreau come to mind. Both of these men were pioneers in championing the benefits of living simply and celebrating the beauty of nature. The reasons for their times of solitude weren't because they were fed up with people and needed to escape into quietness. The quietness they sought was to find even more creative energy within. Thoreau wrote:

I went to the woods because I wished to live deliberately, to front only the essential facts of life, and see if I could not learn what it had to teach, and not, when I came to die, discover that I had not lived. I did not wish to live what was not life, living is so dear; nor did I wish to practice resignation, unless it was quite necessary. I wanted to live deep and suck out all the marrow of life, to live so sturdily and Spartan-like as to put to rout all that was not life, to cut a broad swath and shave close, to drive life into a corner, and reduce it to its lowest terms, and, if it proved to be mean, why then to get the whole and genuine meanness of it, and publish its meanness to the world; or if it were sublime, to know it by experience, and be able to give a true account of it in my next excursion.

Thoreau died in 1862, 30 years before John Muir was born. Wouldn't it have been interesting to go on a camping trip with the two of them? Muir has been called "The Father of Our National Parks System" because of his tremendous efforts to protect our wild areas. He tramped throughout California's Sierra Nevada and wrote, "Climb the mountains and get their good tidings. Nature's peace will flow into you as sunshine flows into trees. The winds will blow their own freshness into you, and the storms their energy, while cares will drop away from you like the leaves of Autumn."

Whether we create community with our fellow human beings or with nature, it's connection that's most important to living fully into the rest of our life's journey.

CHAPTER 8

— • —

WHY BOTHER? DEALING WITH DEPRESSION AND ISOLATION

For Age, with stealing steps,
Hath clawed me with his clutch.

~Thomas Lord Vaux

Between 1937 and 2012, an estimated 1,400 bodies were recovered of people who had jumped off the Golden Gate Bridge into the freezing waters below - 21 people committed suicide in 2021 alone. Life is hard and for some life is unbearably hard. One of my elderly clients said recently, "Why bother! Life is too hard - I really don't know why I'm still here - I'd rather not be." This widower had lost the woman he had loved for over 48 years. The complications of aging were complicated even more by the burden of grief.

I sometimes find myself thinking that life seems so much harder now that I'm old. At times, I can echo the sentiment, "Why bother?" Whether for a lack of physical or mental energy, it's tempting to simply avoid daily tasks and grudgingly go through the motions of keeping body and soul together. Then I remind myself that life was never easy. Growing up wasn't easy. Raising kids, earning a living, finding and keeping friends, staying healthy - none of that was easy. Back then I remember having energy, my body worked, and I remember feeling enthusiastic about the future. What happened, what went wrong? Nothing – I simply got old.

I don't hate being old. It has some advantages. Most of my life's problems have been solved. I got an education, married a great wife, finished raising children, and had a rewarding career. All of life's questions have been answered, even the question of where I'll be buried. I have much more free time to do things I enjoy. I feel very grateful – so why complain? Because feeling grateful doesn't help me walk up flights of stairs without getting winded. It doesn't help me to keep my weight off or like what I see when I look in the mirror.

Even though life is easier in some ways, it can still feel harder. That may be because I've forgotten how hard it had been. Maybe I simply don't have the mental energy I used to have. Mental energy, according to the website Healthline, is a "mood state where you feel productive, motivated, and prepared to get things done." Yes. I do remember what that felt like. The problem is that it seems to come and go – mostly go. Remember the poem, "My get up and go, got up and went"? Look it up, it's fun. It's also true. If you don't believe it, just watch kids run in the park – for no reason at all – just because they want to.

My elderly client has often repeated this to me: "It's hardest in the morning. I reach over to her side of the bed as I always have. But she isn't there." Picturing that loss, the image will break your heart. Loss can be a terrible thing. There is no true antidote for it and no effective cure.

My client comes in regularly just to talk about his partner of 48 years. He misses her terribly. He says it helps to talk about her. There are neurological reasons for the pain and neurological reasons for why talking helps. The three psychiatrists who wrote *A General Theory of Love* note, "When somebody loses his partner and says a part of him is gone, he is more right than he thinks. A portion of his neural activity depends on the presence of that other living brain. Without it, the electric interplay that makes up him has changed."

It seems counterintuitive. Many people imagine that talking about loss will only make the pain worse. They're right – it does. But worse than talking about the pain is not talking about it. Grief therapists and grief support groups exist to help patients heal. They do that by encouraging people to talk about their loss. The neurological process at work is similar to the process of surgically removing a piece jagged metal after a battle. You can't pretend it doesn't hurt and you can't simply place a bandage over it. It has to be removed. When you talk about a painful experience, especially loss, recounting the loss will evoke memory. Memory will evoke emotion, and when emotion surfaces into awareness, it can be neurologically metabolized. Catharsis is the term often used for the release of these painful emotions. Grief is a primary emotion for humans. I'll discuss other primary emotions below. Grieving is the energy to let go of a loss. The loss may be of a person, or a time of your life, a valued experience, or valued possession. What do you do when your house burns down or is carried away by flood or a tornado? You thank God that everyone you love is still alive but you grieve for the memories and cherished possessions that were lost.

What's Good About Feeling Bad?

Allowing yourself to feel fully the emotions of loss will help you to move forward toward acceptance of that loss. Eventually it won't hurt so bad. There is no other way. Yes, you can try not to think about; you can avoid talking about the loss. But the pain won't go away. It will surface in other ways. Far too many veterans have returned from combat not wanting to talk about what they experienced. That's easy to understand. Some of these experiences were unimaginably horrifying. Who wants to talk about them?

What's good about feeling bad is that if you permit the emotions and let yourself talk about them. It's much less likely that the emotions will go underground. In the movie *American Sniper*, the actor portraying Chris Kyle, who returned from four tours in Iraq, shows us what it looks like when emotions go underground. He is sullen, withdrawn, sometimes hostile and angry. He has a hard time relating to his wife and child. When a Veteran Affairs psychiatrist asks him if he is haunted by the things he did, Kyle's response is that he is haunted by all the guys he couldn't save. The psychiatrist encourages Kyle to help other returning soldiers, and in the support groups that Kyle leads, he is finally able to adjust to his civilian life with his wife and children.

War Wounds

A client of mine said that her father was unpredictable – sometimes he was loving and attentive and sometimes he was irrationally angry and abusive. Now, in her 70s, my client still has a habit of too swiftly eating her dinner, a habit she formed to avoid the likelihood that she or another family member would be yelled or hit during dinner. Her mother said that the war had changed her husband. She had married a sweet farm boy. He returned from war emotionally crippled. After World War II, there wasn't yet a clear understanding of the long-term effects of Post-Traumatic Stress Disorder or the ready recourses that are currently available to treat the disorder. In 1994, the 50th anniversary of D-Day was dramatized on television. My client said that her father would sit and watch program after program about the war and weep and weep. These were tears that had not been shed for 50 years, tears that were waiting inside. My client, in addition to eating her dinner too fast, has an exaggerated startle response, and difficulty trusting. She too is a war victim – the victim of her father's untold story. Untold stories about pain and loss drive emotions underground where they can reemerge, unpredictably, in angry outbursts, depression, and emotional isolation. These emotions and their untold stories can, and do, affect generations.

Males in general have a particularly hard time discussing emotions. Terrence Real wrote a book with the perfect title for a book on male depression: *I Don't Want to Talk About It* (1998). I frequently ask the males in my classes, how many of them would have felt comfortable in middle school expressing hurt feelings to other males. No one raises their hands. Deborah Tannen wrote the book *You Just Don't Understand, Women and Men in Conversation*, published in 2007. A sociolinguist, Tannen spent years researching how males and females are socialized to communicate. Her research concluded that boys are typically allowed to communicate and behave more competitively, while girls are encouraged to be more cooperative. Things may have changed some since Tannen did her research, but I'm still not seeing any raised hands from the males in my classroom.

If Tannen is correct and girls are socialized to be more cooperative, this means they have permission to be more vulnerable with each other. This explains why, if someone hurts a girl's feelings in middle school, she is much more likely than a boy to seek out a friend for comfort. She can talk about her hurt feelings and anticipate her friend being supportive and comforting. What a difference this is from what a boy anticipates. Boys who are vulnerable with other boys are frequently called derogative names like "sissy," or worse, and made to feel ashamed about being open with their feelings. This feeling of shame, in proximity to being vulnerable, creates the habit of "I don't want to talk about it," a habit that can last a lifetime, and a habit that can render men less successful in intimate relationships.

The most common complaint I hear from wives about their husbands is that they don't know how to, or don't want to talk about their feelings. In addition, husbands can be very impatient when their wives want to talk to them about their emotions. I see this as a hangover from having little tolerance or training for dealing with other's emotions earlier in life. So much of my work as a marriage counselor is helping to undo bad habits and to encouraging more emotional access, vulnerability, and expressiveness.

For some fortunate men, the habit can be broken. Developing close friendships with other guys can heal the tendency to feel shame about one's emotions. For so many of us older guys, it still isn't easy. We can sit around eating donuts or nachos and talk about all kinds of things, but rarely what's going on with us emotionally. We can play a round of golf and have a few beers, but we don't really know each other. I suppose that's okay. Getting together with other guys doesn't always have to be a therapy session. But who *can* we talk to?

Surfacing the Wounds

I think that many of us older adults are depressed because we have no genuinely close friends, and, yes, that is especially true for men. I've already written about why it is so important to talk about feelings. Yet so often we don't even know what's going on deep inside. It isn't until we start to talk with a person we trust and with whom we can be completely open that uncomfortable emotions can surface into awareness. Of course, seeing a therapist works, but it also works to have someone with whom you can share deeply, going to emotional places that have been tucked away and perhaps hidden for years and talking about the hurts. A genuinely close friend will feel honored and compassionate when you trust them that much.

People say that it helps to get things "off your chest." We've discussed the neurological processes that explain how that happens. Bartenders and hairdressers also know that it helps to get things off your chest and may be surprisingly effective in the kinds of active listening that help their customers feel better. Are you a good listener? Do you have the courage and patience to go deep with a close friend and, for a time, step onto their path with them? It may take courage and patience. It may be a painful journey. You need to understand and accept that for both you and your close friend, it can be good to allow yourself to feel bad. It can be good to allow painful memories and emotions to surface into awareness where they can be felt and healed. People often apologize for tearing up in social contexts. Of course - the idea is not to burden others with your own emotions. But, with your close friends, that's exactly what you should allow yourself to do.

The word "love" can be both a noun and a verb. As a verb, love is about behavior. I shared earlier M. Scott Peck's definition of love in his book *The Road Less Traveled* - that love is the willingness to extend oneself in order to facilitate one's own or another's spiritual growth. By spiritual growth, I think Peck means "ultimate well-being." Truly loving someone is, of course, much more than an emotion - it is the work of extending oneself, even in the face of challenges, discomfort, and pain. The apostle Paul got it right when he wrote a letter to a church in

Corinth, Greece. Paul said that love (according to the King James Bible) "suffers long." The Greek word is translated as "patience" in modern Bibles but the translation is more impactful when the word describes the inevitable and unavoidable connection between love and suffering.

More About Emotions

If there is value in discussing emotions, then it's important to understand them. Primary emotions are vital for our survival. Grief is the energy to let go, to grieve a loss, and move toward acceptance and peace. Anger helps to motivate us for self-protection. It is also the energy needed to change an intolerable situation. Fear alerts us to danger and prompts us to take preventive action. These are powerful emotions, along with courage (the energy we need to face danger), love (the energy to forge and secure attachments), and joy (the amazing sense of ecstatic well-being).

"Neural Integration" is the term used for the metabolic work the brain does to neutralize the intensity of emotional memory. It's an amazing and wonderful ability the brain has of transforming and integrating (healing) emotional pain. Look up that term, and marvel at how the brain, in addition to the body, is miraculously able to heal hurts. Most people have heard the term "catharsis." The Oxford Dictionary says that catharsis is the "process of releasing, and thereby providing relief from, strong or repressed emotions." When you tell someone your story and find yourself feeling emotion - anger, sadness, anxiety - you have two choices: to *access* or *avoid*. Again, in social situations when you'd rather not burden others with your emotions, you'll often select to avoid those uncomfortable emotions and change the topic. However, if you're talking to a counselor, close friend, family member, priest, minister, or rabbi, or anyone you trust, take a deep breath and face the feelings. Don't avoid them. Allowing emotions to surface into awareness will facilitate catharsis and neural integration. Confession, it turns out, is very good for the soul.

Counselors help people to practice both expressiveness and containment. Sometimes it's good to open up and sometimes it's better to remain silent. A mature person knows when to do each. I've noticed over the years that in a relationship, one person often needs to practice being a more open talker and the other person being a better listener. What have you noticed in your relationships?

From Grief to Gratitude

I had another appointment recently with a dear elderly white-haired widow. I've seen her now for nearly twelve months. She cried during our first appointment as she talked about the terrible pain of losing her husband of sixty years. She said the same thing my elderly widower had said – that a part of her was gone. Both had perfectly voiced that passage from *A General Theory of Love* which explains the neurophysiology of loss. Both of these fortunate people had experienced deep and profound connections with the partner they had loved so dearly.

For the first time since I began to see her, she seemed relaxed and happy. "I think I've turned a corner," she explained. "When I look at my husband's photo on my nightstand and kiss him goodnight or good morning, I no longer feel twisted up inside with missing him. It seems that I'm able to spend more time thinking about the wonderful times we had together, the trips, the holidays, enjoying raising our children." I won't use the term beatific, but her smile simply seemed at peace. "You were right," she said, "lately I have been able to spend much more time feeling grateful for the life we had together. I have been able to realize what a gift he had been in my life, and how blessed I am." She has answered the question from the title of the chapter – *why bother?* – by dealing with her isolation from her beloved husband by practicing gratitude, something I've advocated throughout this book. When you feel isolated, lonely, or depressed, reminding yourself of the gifts and blessings of your long life thus far may turn your emotions around and bring you a sense of peaceful acceptance of the inevitable losses and hardships of aging and beyond.

CHAPTER 9

—— • ——

A GOOD DEATH OR
A BAD DEATH?

And come he slow, or come he fast,
It is but Death who comes at last.

~Sir Walter Scott

A Bad Death

We don't have many, but we do have some choices about how and when we will die. Of course, I'm referring to good and bad lifestyle choices. According to the American Cancer Society, deaths related to smoking have been on the decline for several years. That's good. People are making better choices about smoking. Obesity and alcohol, however, may still contribute to cancer deaths and other major health problems – but we already know all of this. We older adults have had it drummed into us for most of our lives that our health is directly related to our lifestyle choices.

So what kinds of bad deaths am I talking about? I'm not talking about the stupid kinds – the kinds of death that can be easily prevented by making better lifestyle choices. I'm talking about the death of the body that directly results from the death of the soul. Recall in Chapter 2, I talked about the nature of the soul. If you're uncomfortable with religious language, I'll make it simple – your soul is the person you are that is not limited to your body. I won't try to explain the difference between your mind, which seems to be related to your brain, which is definitely a part of your body, and your soul. Let's just say that your soul is that part of you that is able to know what is ultimately valuable – your ability to know the best choices for your life, and the courage to make those choices.

We come into life and we go out of life. We've talked already about how the first half of life is mainly devoted to developing an ego, which is your ability to relate successfully to the outer world of convention and expectations. Ideally, you've achieved most of what you thought would be important by midlife, somewhere between ages 40 and 50. After midlife, if you're healthy psychologically, you are less concerned about what your ego wants and more concerned about what is truly valuable – what your soul wants.

Too many people get stuck in midlife, however. Either they haven't figured out what is truly valuable or they have a hard time letting go of what they valued in their younger days. Sporty cars and plastic surgery may maintain the pretense of youthfulness, but if you get stuck in midlife and fail to pay attention, you may not discover what is truly valuable in life while you're still able to make better choices. What is worse than being stuck? Going in the wrong direction. I'll give you a few illustrations of people who went in the wrong direction.

My favorite illustration is Captain Ahab from Herman Melville's book *Moby Dick*. Ahab had a very bad death. Below is a painting I did of the Pequod just sighting the white whale Moby Dick in the distance. The captain of the Pequod should have been grateful for the opportunity to earn a good living by filling his hull with the precious whale oil that would light the lamps of New England, but he went the wrong direction – the direction of his ego's need for vengeance against the whale that took off his leg. If your life is centered around vengeance, you will have a bad death. Like Ahab, you will be tied to the object of your hatred and it will take you under.

Bad deaths are about going in the wrong direction, one of which is inflated pride. I wouldn't want to be shot and hung upside down for public viewing like the Italian dictator Benito Mussolini. Neither did Adolf Hitler, so he ordered that his body be burned following his suicide. Ahab, Adolf, and Benito went in the wrong direction because of inflated pride, like Lucifer in the Bible who announced, "I will be like the most high!" Lucifer's pride pushed him to want to be equal with God - never a good idea. When Starbuck appealed to Ahab, "To be enraged with a dumb thing, Captain Ahab, seems blasphemous," Ahab blasted back, "Talk not to me of blasphemy man, I'd strike the sun if it insulted me." Ahab, Adolf, and Benito allowed their egos to take the helm. Inflated pride and unbridled egos make poor helmsmen.

There are certainly many other illustrations I could recount, but these three, along with Lucifer, are sufficient to make my point. Closer to home, you'll be shocked when you look at Wikipedia's list of over 700 celebrities who died accidentally or intentionally because of drugs and alcohol. Among the list are too many from our generation - Jim,

Jimi, and Janice, Marilyn and Elvis. No doubt there are reasons for these deaths that are hard for us to understand, but I can't imagine that any of these creative people would have wanted this kind of death.

Allow me a distinction here. I'm not talking about painful deaths. There are so many painful ways to die, too many to count. These are deaths due to accidents, violence, and illness. We can all pray that we die without too much physical or emotional pain. What I'm talking about in this chapter is bad deaths. A truly bad and tragic death results from the death of the soul, and sometimes ushers evil into the world. Dr. Laura Sockul wrote a paper titled "The Man Who Mistook a Whale for Pure Evil: A Diagnostic Assessment of Captain Ahab." She correctly diagnosed Ahab with malignant narcissism. Being a narcissist is bad enough because you're trying to play God, but the malignant kind takes the whole crew, the whole country, and the whole world in the wrong direction. This kind of bad death is one in which you are remembered for the evil you inflicted and for what you destroyed. You don't want to have that kind of death.

Why would someone go in the wrong direction with their life? You might blame parents. You might blame society. You might blame God. Yet, sometimes, no one is to blame. We simply make bad choices. People make bad choices for many reasons. There is (or should be) a quiet voice inside of you. You've heard it even if you've never listened closely. When you do listen closely, you'll recognize bad choices – the choices that take you in the wrong direction, away from life toward death, and potentially a bad death. A bad death is one in which you may be remembered for betraying love, neglecting kindness, hoarding, and hiding and running away from the good you could have done. Or you were just lazy about the value of your life.

You are not Ahab, Adolf, or Benito. You're (hopefully!) not in the category of malignant narcissists. You haven't gone in the wrong direction with your life. You haven't left a legacy of (only) bad choices. However, you may still have the wrong kind of death if you are not remembered at all. You made no impact on anyone. You simply did your time. You did your job and minded your own business. Make sure it's a good business while you still can. Recall from Charles Dickens' *A Christmas Carol* what the ghost of Jacob Marley said to Ebenezer Scrooge about minding your own business: "'Business!?'" Marley exclaimed. 'The common welfare was my business; charity, mercy, forbearance, and benevolence, were, all my business. The dealings of my trade were but a drop of water in the comprehensive ocean of my business!'" Earning a living is good – being a kind and benevolent person in the dealings of your business is best.

When Choices Become Chains

Marley went on to say that his penance, after death, was to wear the chains he forged in life. He made them "link by link, and yard by yard." When do choices become chains? Ask an alcoholic or a heroin addict. Ask someone whose day is fixated on the ups and downs of the stock market. Ask anyone who is chasing a whale and going in the wrong direction. A much better question to ask now is how to reverse course.

"Man overboard!" calls for immediate action. The officer on deck will order the helmsman to put the rudder hard over to keep the propeller from hitting the man in the water and then affect a "Williamson turn," putting the ship on a reverse course to come alongside the man. I recall from experience that turning and slowing a naval vessel takes a long time. So does casting off chains. The ego wants what the ego wants and is willing to risk drowning if necessary.

It takes time, but the chains of bad choices can be broken. They are broken by changing course. No one is doomed to a bad death. What does your soul want? Unless you are gravely wounded psychologically, your soul wants to experience life. Listen to it. Your soul wants connection and meaning. Where can you find that? Look around – possibilities are all around you. According to Gene Cohen who wrote *The Mature Mind*, the first step may be to "choose something appealing and challenging – something you'll have to work at." I would add, something that feeds your soul and, ideally, something that may border on becoming a benevolent obsession – a positive, life-enhancing obsession to make a difference in the lives of people. Because it often takes a new addiction to break an old one; find who and what needs you.

Fear and Laziness

These are the two main reasons why people choose not to change course. People are afraid to make major life changes for many reasons – fear of being a failure, fear of the unexpected, fear that the change will require too much effort, fear of change itself. Some people are comfortable with their bad habits. Change requires effort and some people are just too lazy or tired. They might not die a bad death, but they may not have ever truly lived. I've said this repeatedly. It isn't too late. It isn't too late to make something of your life, to find meaning and connection. This is what your soul wants: to leave behind something of value.

You may be tired. You have been busy doing life and taking care of business. The great thing about being older is now, hopefully, you have choices you didn't have earlier in life. If you don't have to work, it might be nice to work somewhere fun. Not long ago I took my family to Disneyland. I've been there many times and didn't need to go on all of the rides - my greatest enjoyment came from hearing how much fun my family was having. I noticed how many older people were working there. They looked like they were enjoying themselves. A good choice in later life is to bring happiness to others. If it's the right kind of work and a pleasing environment, the energy for the work is *in* the work. There are certain types of volunteer work available where you can set your own pace and your own hours. I talked with a 78-year-old man recently who is still very active in his community and place of worship. He will probably live well into his 90s - he has good reasons to stay alive. So don't tell yourself that there's nothing more you can do with your life. Listen to your soul. It is still youthful.

Bitterness and Isolation

Bitterness and isolation are lethal. I have a friend, a recovering alcoholic, who told me that bitterness will kill you. He knows. He had friends who kept drinking to numb themselves from resentments and bitterness. Only one is still alive. Ebenezer Scrooge must have been very bitter. Dickens tells us that Scrooge's mother died giving him birth and his resentful father sent Ebenezer away to live in a boarding school. Early in life, Scrooge made the decision to retreat, to cut himself off from the possibility of feeling alive. He anesthetized himself by chaining himself to a life of isolation, and lived to hoard money. It took being visited by four ghosts to terrorize him into changing the direction of his life. Fear can promote change – when it isn't too late to change. Scrooge woke up on Christmas morning a changed man.

The problem for many of us are memories that won't go away – like a piece of shrapnel in the soul. Shrapnel, that jagged piece of metal, can enter the body in places that are too dangerous to surgically remove. My son-in-law who works in an intercity emergency room told me that in many instances, surgeons decide to leave bullets in place. More damage is done by trying to remove them. But shrapnel in the soul is a different matter. When a bitter memory is touched, the pain can be excruciating. What do you do when that happens?

The surgery of the soul requires the work of forgiveness. Step 8 and 9 of the 12 steps of Alcoholics Anonymous ask addicts to make a list of all persons they have harmed and become willing to make amends to them, and to make direct amends to such people wherever possible, except if it would injure them or others. This means finding the humility and courage to ask for forgiveness from others and to be able to receive forgiveness for yourself. Recovering alcoholics know intimately that healing from resentment and bitterness is among the most difficult work of maintaining sobriety. It is also the most important work. They understand that without the work of forgiveness, healing can't happen, and without healing, recovery won't happen. This is an axiom that has been tested again and again by thousands of men and women in recovery. As they say in meetings: "It works if you work it."

Some people are not courageous. Some lack humility. Some feel too ashamed to ask for forgiveness. Some people allow their resentments to define them. They feel naked and vulnerable without the armor of their resentments. They hold onto anger at others, anger at life, and anger at God. Any of these can steel a person with the black energy needed to buffer one's soul against the pain of having been gravely wounded by life. Such a person finds solace in isolation, clutching resentments and nursing bitterness in dark corners.

We've already discussed how isolation can be a health hazard, and how it can lead to depression. We talked about how males, more than females, are reluctant to deal with depression and its underlying causes. A 2016 World Health Organization survey of 793,000 suicides worldwide reported that the majority of those suicides were male, and the BBC reported that in Australia, where macho stoicism may be high, males are three and a half times more likely to commit suicide than in the U.S. Bitterness and isolation can kill you, and that's not a good death because it could have been prevented. To prevent a bad death, besides staying physically healthy, it's important to make sure you're connected to good friends, a service organization, or a community of faith. You need people around to care about you and for you to care about.

Connection and a Good Death

The antidote to isolation is connection. There is an old Kingston Trio song called *Desert Pete*. According to the song, the thirsty singer found a well and a pump in the middle of the desert with a note from Desert Pete saying that he left a bottle of just enough water to prime the pump. Desert Pete encouraged those at the well to have faith and belief, and to leave the bottle full for others. Similarly, priming the pump of connection takes faith and courage. I know that it's hard to believe at times, but most people are friendly and actually do care. Find a local place of worship – it doesn't matter what kind, or a community center. There is usually someone there you can talk to. Prime the pump. Find the courage and faith you need to reach out. It may save your life, and it will certainly make it a better one.

So what is a good death? A good death is the fruit of making good choices – it's the result of the choices you make to value yourself and others. A good life is not a perfect life, because none of us can avoid making some wrong, perhaps even bad, decisions. We may have been careless at times, and we may have unintentionally hurt others. Hopefully, we forgave those who harmed us, and we asked for forgiveness and made amends. We did the best we could to get back on the right track. Best of all, we did our best to bring some love, kindness, and value into the world. A good death comes from making choices that result in a good life.

CHAPTER 10

• •

YOUR MEMORIAL SERVICE

Fill to me the parting glass. And drink a health whate'er befalls.
Then gently rise and softly call good night and joy be to you all.
~Ancient Scottish Farewell

In the last chapter, we talked about what a good death would look like. Now let's turn to look at a good memorial service.

There's a memorial service scene in the movie *Waking Ned Devine* that I recommend you watch. In it, a close friend of the deceased says this: "The words that are spoken at a funeral are spoken too late for the man that is dead. What a wonderful thing it would be to visit your own funeral, to sit at the front and hear what was said, and maybe say a few things yourself." I like that idea. If you were to attend your own memorial service, what would you like to hear? How would you like to be remembered? Is it ever too early to write out what you would like at your memorial service?

You're the one who's departing so it would make sense that you should get to choose your sendoff. But for many that may be wishful thinking. Every culture has its own way of saying goodbye and families have their own traditions, so you may not have much of a say in the matter. In addition, you may not have an opportunity or willingness to discuss the topic, or your family may not want to talk with you about it (how morbid, they might think). But if you're in a part of the world that permits it, your family doesn't mind, and you've given it some thought, it would be nice to choose how you'd like to be remembered and how you'd like people to say goodbye.

What is a Memorial Service?

There are many answers to that question depending on your culture and religion. But in general, a service of remembrance is a safe time and place for tears and memories. From a psychological perspective, people need closure – they need to grieve. They need catharsis, a release of emotions, a way of letting go, which often comes in the form of tears. In some cultures, tears and catharsis are mandatory on behalf of the departed. A memorial service is also, literally, a time to remember. The last memorial service I attended had a slide presentation of the person's life. Photos and videos have become popular in many memorial services. In addition to tears and memories, people also enjoy light-hearted moments of endearing and even humorous stories.

In Christian cultures, it's common now to use the term "a celebration of life." That is certainly the idea in the celebrated funerals popular in New Orleans and in traditional Irish wakes. While it's less common in modern Ireland, the "wake" was created in the days when people who were suffering from unknown illnesses might appear dead only to recover later. The family and friends would sit vigil during the night to make sure the "deceased" didn't wake. Music and drinking would help to pass the time. There's a fun favorite Irish drinking song about a wake called "Finnegan's Wake." Tim Finnegan was supposed to be dead after he fell from a ladder and landed on his head. The lyrics go:

> They rolled him up in a nice clean sheet
> And laid him out upon the bed
> With a gallon of whiskey at his feet
> And a barrel of porter at his head

A ruckus among the mourners knocked over the whiskey which scattered over Tim:

Tim revives, see how he rises
Timothy rising from the bed
Said "Whirl your whiskey around like blazes
Thundering Jesus, do you think I'm dead?"

Sitting shiva is another cultural tradition, the traditional Jewish way of mourning. The custom may have originated, like the wake, to ensure the deceased was actually gone – also an important part of the grieving process. For orthodox Jews, sitting shiva would last for seven days. For reformed Jews, the time may be less. In Japan, family and friends gather for a typical Buddhist or Shinto ceremony conducted by a priest. The beautiful 2008 film, *Departures*, contains an extraordinarily touching depiction of a formal Japanese funeral service in which the mourners are gathered to observe the careful and dignified washing of the deceased in preparation for cremation. In Mexico and other Catholic countries, in addition to a vigil lasting an evening or a few days prior to the funeral, the deceased is also celebrated in a typical Catholic mass. When we travel to Italy to visit family, we notice a common Catholic tradition in the smaller villages to have photos of the recently deceased posted near the church daily. Bells ring slowly and somberly, honoring the life of each deceased.

Saying goodbye to a loved one involves family and friends, memories and stories, and sometimes photos as guests pay their respects to the family and are often treated to food and drink following the service. Prayers are offered by a minister, priest, imam, or rabbi and, as I said, a service of remembrance is a safe place to cry, to pray, to tell stories, and to experience the love and support of loved ones.

My father and mother opted for an informal memorial service. Many of Dad and Mom's friends at church and elsewhere were invited to a celebration of life. My father's memorial gathering was held in the church social hall and my mother's at their home. Later family members gathered for brief graveside services. In both memorial services, people who knew my parents had lots of stories to tell, many endearing, some hilarious. Dad and Mom were both elderly and said that they had had a good life, so the time of remembrance was exactly what they would have wanted, an opportunity for friends and family to gather and share stories.

I'm sure that my parents had little idea of the power of their legacy regarding death. More than planning and paying in advance for their final resting place, they both told me exactly what they wished for a memorial service, where their important papers were located, including the family trust, insurance information, various receipts, and so forth. As my mom grew weaker, she made sure to reassure me that she was ready and that she loved us all. Similarly, the last words I heard my father say was that he had had a good life, and that he had married his best friend. How much easier it was for my two brothers and me to sign the necessary paperwork at Forest Lawn Memorial Park. Everything had already been taken care of. The point of this story is to encourage us older folks not to be timid about letting people know how we would like to be remembered. We will be remembered one way or another. It would be good if our friends and family remembered that we faced the end of our life peacefully and courageously, that we planned and paid for our funeral arrangements, and that we weren't afraid to talk about our life story as well as the end of our life.

You've noticed that throughout this book, I've offered various reasons for accepting and facing the end of your life, not avoiding thinking about your final wishes, and discussing those wishes with family members and/or friends. You may frequently get some sort of opposition like, "Oh, Dad, you'll live forever." Yes, it's an uncomfortable topic but don't let people off the hook. If they refuse to have any conversations, write out your wishes for your burial and memorial service and put them in an envelope with other important papers. Do it while you are still healthy enough. It will encourage folks who love you to know that you've made plans for that day in the future, and hopefully, your courage will inspire theirs, as my parents' courage inspired me.

A Tale of Two Memorial Services

I was 16 when my maternal grandfather died. We flew back east to attend his memorial service. I didn't want to go. I wanted to remember Grandpa the way he was and I had never been to a funeral before. But I'm glad I went. Reverend McNutt knew my grandfather well and told some heartwarming and humorous stories about him. Everyone was enjoying the stories and everyone was quietly crying. That's another reason I didn't want to go – I had never cried in public and didn't want to. But everyone was crying so I did too. The tears seemed different than I thought they would be. They didn't feel morbid or hopeless. They were tears of love. Reverend McNutt concluded his talk with an image of Grandpa sailing off into the horizon. People on this side of the ocean would say, "There he goes." But people on the other side would joyously say, "Here he comes!"

After the service, we went back to the house for some refreshments. Relatives and friends from all over the neighboring area were in attendance so they had brought sandwiches, salads, and desserts to share. This wasn't at all what I had expected. It seemed more like a family reunion and, in a sense, it was. It was a reunion of people who knew and loved Grandpa. It was truly a celebration of a life. What I remember the most was the peaceful presence of my grandmother. I had never before experienced the true strength of the Christian faith. She embodied it. She knew she would see her husband again and, through her loss, she radiated hope and confident peace. A memorial service is a time to grieve and a time to remember. It's also a time to embrace and celebrate the ties of love.

That was my first experience of a funeral and memorial service. Here's one of the latest. In July of 2021, I officiated at a memorial service of a 94-year-old man. It was a beautiful experience. I had known George since 1976. It was easy to say good things about him, but what people enjoyed the most were the stories. So many people stood up during the service and had poignant or humorous stories about George. George told me before he died that he had had a good life, and the stories that were told about George and his family confirmed that. He married a wonderful woman and had many great years together. He raised two children, enjoyed his grandchildren, had a rewarding teaching career for many years, and was active in his church and community. He touched people's lives with his genuine interest and kindness. Yes, I would say that George had a good life. It doesn't get much better. All of us who knew George valued this service of remembrance. If you would like to be a person whom people say good things about at a memorial service – be that person.

The Importance of a Time and Place for Grieving

Grieving is tremendously important. Tears help people to move forward toward acceptance. Recall that Elizabeth Kubler Ross wrote *On Death and Dying* in 1969 where she discussed the main stages of the grief process: denial, anger, bargaining, depression, and acceptance. If you are a grief counselor you often hear, "I can't believe he's gone!" "Why didn't God intervene?" "If only I had said something." "I don't know what I'll do now that she's gone." These are common sayings representing the first stages of the grieving process. Grief counselors will also tell you that the stages are not necessarily linear. People can have a hard time adjusting and alternate between anger and depression, asking why their prayers (bargaining with God) weren't answered, or what could or should have been done to prevent the loss. There are no fixed rules about how long grieving takes place. But there is one clear and fixed rule: people need to grieve a loss. Sadness and tears are the energy required to let go. Without doing the work of grieving, a person may become stuck in bitterness, anger, or depression. So as much as we want a memorial service to be a celebration of our lives, it's important to make this also a time and place for grieving.

From my experience, a great way to remember someone and process your grief over losing them is to tell stories about them. People who come to me for therapy after a loss are often surprised at my instructions. "Tell me about them," I ask. And what unfolds from that simple request are the precious memories of a time of love – golden moments that stir the emotions and stories of past joys or the painful stories that always accompany life. It's painful to recall those times of love and joy, on the one hand, or to remember past hurts and struggles on the other. That's as it should be. They are treasures to keep close or challenging emotions that need to be faced. But at the same time, those memories bring the emotions close to the surface where the brain can do its metabolic work, processing and digesting the energy inside of the emotions leading to a process psychologists call "neural integration" – a release and lessening of the pain of loss. The grief process is a painful imperative for surviving a loss, letting go, and remaining fully alive, and a memorial service serves as an important time and place to work that process, to cry those good tears that show you've loved someone well and have suffered a loss.

I once played the Scottish song "Ae Fond Kiss" for my wife. She got mad at me for doing it. She doesn't like to cry. Listening to the lines of a poem by Robert Burns that were put to music, I can see why she was crying.

Had we never loved sae kindly
Had we never loved sae blindly
Nor never met, nor never parted
We would never have been so broken-hearted
Fare thee weel, my first and fairest
Fare thee weel, my best and dearest
Thine be like joy and treasure…
Peace, enjoyment, love and pleasure
Mmm, ae fond kiss, and then we sever
Ae fareweel alas, forever
Deep in heart-wrung tears I'll pledge thee
Warring sighs and groans I'll wage thee

"I'll play this at your funeral," she said, "but I don't want to hear it again until then!"

Music has long been played at memorial services to express and invite the grieving process. Music has also been written for that same purpose, like "Ae Fond Kiss." Another example is Johannes Brahms' "German Requiem." In 1865, one year after his beloved mother died, he composed one of the most moving and powerful requiems ever penned. He was 32 years old. One year later, Brahms had written most of the text for the first movement of *Ein Deutsch's Requiem*, music based on the beatitudes (Jesus' sermon on the mount):

> Blessed are they that mourn, for they shall be comforted. They who sow in tears, shall reap in joy. Go forth and cry, bearing precious seed, and come with joy bearing their sheaves.

No doubt Brahms grasped the promise that his mourning and his tears over the loss of his mother would, in time, translate into a final acceptance and perhaps later, even joy in her memory. I can imagine that Brahms, like all true artists, found creative energy from his suffering and from that suffering forged a timeless memorial.

It's in the second movement that Brahms exposes the true horror of death. The text is taken from 1st Peter 1:24, from Luther's Bible: "For all flesh is as grass." Death isn't pretty. It's unrelenting, coming too soon for many, and without discrimination. Human life is like grass – the grass withers, the flowers fade and, in a moment, we are gone. This second movement is a funeral procession – a slow cadenced march to the grave. You are drawn along in the funeral procession accompanied by the mournful beating of drums. The first part of the movement is terrifying with its relentless grip, moving you along. But high above the procession, the altos and sopranos sing a lullaby – a lullaby that only Brahms could write, from the text of Isaiah 51:11. The lullaby is woven into the funeral march with its promise that death is not the end:

> The redeemed of the Lord will come again and come to Zion with a shout; eternal joy shall be upon her head; They shall take joy and gladness, and sorrow and sighing must depart.

In my imagination, I see Brahms, perhaps in tears, unwilling to beautify death. It is awful. It is painful. It comes for those we love – it comes for us all. But for Brahms, the suffering and pain will eventually cease. In the fourth movement, Brahms reassures himself of his mother's end, at rest in the house of the Lord. From Psalms 84, Brahms frames this movement as another lullaby.

How lovely are thy dwelling places, O Lord of Hosts! My soul requires and yearns for the courts of the Lord; My body and soul rejoice in the living God. Blessed are they that dwell in thy house; they praise you forever.

The fifth movement, from the Gospel of John 16:22, is the most poignant. A solo soprano sings as if it is Brahms' mother herself addressing him:

You now have sorrow; but I shall see you again and your heart shall rejoice and your joy no one shall take from you. Behold me: I have had for a little time toil and torment, and now have found great consolation. I will console you, as one is consoled by his mother.

There are times when it is good to cry. Brahms' requiem is what I listen to when I need to. There is a great deal of pain in the world. In a recent example, viewing the empty strollers representing the infants that perished in the Russian war against Ukraine, the bombed-out cities, and the countless displaced families can make anyone cry. It's important not to always run away from being exposed to pain. It's important at times to let yourself feel that pain, and perhaps at no time is it more important than at a memorial service and funeral, when we are in touch with our own broken hearts. My elderly client who lost his wife of 48 years told me that his suffering had softened his heart. He subsequently volunteered at his synagogue to be of service to others.

Planning Your Memorial Service

Planning your own memorial service can be an act of service to your loved ones, allowing them to focus in the aftermath of your death not on the minutia of event planning, but instead on processing their own grief, their broken-heartedness. Of course, you realize that you are planning an event where you won't be the host. That's okay – you can still plan something that will be meaningful and memorable for the people that you care about. You may select to have your memorial service at the place of worship you regularly attend. You may have it at the cemetery, memorial park, or funeral home. You may decide to have a service at the beach, on the golf course, or under a magnificent oak. It is customary in the United States to have both a memorial service and a graveside service. However, the memorial service is usually not held at the gravesite. Consequently, it doesn't especially matter where or when you have your memorial service. The memorial service often features a spiritual leader who officiates the service, and who invites someone to give a eulogy and gives others a chance to say a few words. Sometimes favorite hymns are sung, passages of scripture or other readings are offered, and a lovely recent tradition is to invite mourners to view slides or videos chosen by the family. Recall that the principal purpose of a service of remembrance is to help people grieve – so viewing scenes from a loved one's life is a sweet way to help people to remember.

Of course, you can allow the people you love to make their own decisions about how to remember and celebrate you, or, you can help them out by planning all this in advance. You can let your family know where you'd like to have the memorial service, and who you would like to officiate it. You can let people close to you know that when you die, you'd love to have them speak a few words, or deliver the eulogy - they would be honored to know that. You can leave a list of the music you'd like to have played, and copies of your favorite passages of scripture or poetry or other text that's sacred to you. My mom wanted her friends to hear the words of the 23rd Psalm. This was one of her favorite psalms and she wanted her friends to be comforted by it. She also loved the hymn, *In the Garden*. The point is not to be shy about inviting family and friends to feel ministered to by what you select to comfort them. You can even prepare the slide show in advance, to save your family and friends from having to dig through old photo albums or folders of digital photographs and make selections while they're in the process of mourning. If what you select invites tears, so much the better.

You might even take a few moments to write out your own eulogy. Does that seem strange? Are you worried that you may be unconsciously inviting death sooner than you'd wish? No, I don't think it's strange. I think it actually may be a good exercise to look at how your life has gone so far and, perhaps, what might be left to do, or maybe good to do. What would you like to say? What would you like people to hear? Keep it in a safe place where you can visit it from time to time and maybe add a few things. And, no, I wouldn't worry about an unconscious death wish – just the opposite, I think it will give you some things to look forward to. In your self-written eulogy, you might want to say something like, "In her late 80s, she had visited every capital in the United States," or "In his early 90s he continued to be active in community service." Thinking about what you would like to say about yourself may inspire you to have something more to say. I have a close friend who told me that she was given the assignment of writing out her eulogy for a college class. No doubt this was a very innovative way of encouraging students to be intentional about their lives.

It's never too late to be intentional about your life, or what happens in the aftermath of your death.

CHAPTER 11

TO TRAVEL WITH DIGNITY

Grace was in all her steps, heaven in her eye.
In every gesture dignity and love.

~John Milton

In the last chapter, I suggested writing your own eulogy as a means of reminding yourself of how you want to travel through the last part of your journey here on earth. In this chapter, I want to talk about traveling with dignity.

It's hard to feel dignified when you're wearing a diaper. We were wearing diapers when we began our lives and we may be wearing them at the end. But don't be confused. Although we now live in bodies that don't work the way they used to, and our aging biology regularly betrays us, we can still have dignity. This chapter holds out the promise that our dignity is not found in what we look like or how life has taken its toll on us - our dignity is found in who we are.

What is Dignity?

What is dignity, what does it look like, and how do you have it? The answer to all three of these questions is the same. Dignity is found in how you treat others. A person with dignity treats everyone alike, as valuable human beings worthy of respect. The Oxford Dictionary states that dignity is:

1. the state or quality of being worthy of honor or respect. "A man of dignity & unbending principle."
2. a composed or serious manner or style. "He bowed with great dignity."
3. a sense of pride in oneself; self-respect. "It was beneath his dignity to shout."

Another example of dignity may be: "the respect paid to an elder member in the family." However, you could also say that as the elder member of the family, you bestow dignity on your family members when you treat them with dignity.

I like all of these definitions, but I think that the best definition of dignity resides in the person you are and how you treat others. This means that even if you're wearing a diaper, you have hair where you don't want it and not where you do, and you hate what you look like in the mirror, you can still have dignity.

Remember when Ronald Reagan was shot? No doubt Reagan sensed that the doctors around him were nervous about having to cut into the leader of the free world. Regan was reported to have taken off his oxygen mask in order to quip, "I hope you're all Republicans!" Some people might not think of that as particularly dignified but, according to my definition, it was exactly that. Even in pain, even with anxiety about what's happening to you, you can still care about how you treat others – in Reagan's case, with levity born of the compassion he may have felt for his surgical team.

To paraphrase the Oxford Dictionary definition again, dignity is having unbending principles, performing courteous acts, and being considerate of others. If you still have your wits about you, even as an older person, you can still have dignity, and you can still have self-respect and pride in yourself. In fact, if that is all you have left, that would be enough.

I Remember Nadesan

Maya Angelou is quoted as saying, "At the end of the day, people won't remember what you said or did, they will remember how you made them feel." There is certainly truth in that, especially if what they say or do makes you feel positive emotions. Without a doubt, when someone treats you in a way that creates the feeling of being accepted and valued, you will likely remember that person.

I still remember Nadesan. He was voted the most popular kid in my high school. Nadesan wasn't a star athlete, or especially noteworthy in ways high school kids are remembered. In high school, Nadesan was a slender young man born in India who, my fellow students would agree, was the soul of dignity. Everyone agreed that Nadesan had that special ability to make you feel as if you were the most important person around. You always had his full attention, and his ability to carefully listen and value everything you said was extraordinary. In this respect Maya Angelou is correct – 56 years later, I still remember Nadesan.

Whom do you recall in your lifetime that you would characterize as having dignity? Why? What qualities stand out in your mind? What stands out in my mind are people with generous and gracious hearts, people who can laugh at themselves, and people who refuse to think too highly of themselves. Do you think that you will be remembered as having dignity? I've said this before – you still have time to be that person.

Dignity is a Direction

I was talking with an elderly gentleman recently. His wife had passed away not long ago and he was wise enough to know that he needed to grieve. One of his friends suggested that he call me as a person he could talk with. I value doing this kind of work – helping people talk about and process their loss and eventually find peace. We were talking about his fears going forward. "I'm not afraid to die," he said, "I'm afraid of being useless and dependent." It sounded to me like he was also afraid of losing his dignity. Of course he was – just like the rest of us.

It helps to bear in mind that dignity is actually a *direction*. What does that mean? When Jesus encouraged an audience on a hill in northern Israel by saying, "Blessed are the pure in heart, for they shall see God," he was echoing Psalm 24:3-4: "Who may ascend the mountain of the LORD? Who may stand in his holy place? The one who has clean hands and a pure heart, who does not trust in an idol or swear by a false god." The apostle Paul, writing to his protégé, Timothy, encourages him to love people with a pure heart, to have a good conscience, and sincere faith. If dignity is how you treat others, it must be acquired by reflecting on your motives, searching with clean hands and a pure heart, and pursuing what is truly valuable. This is a direction.

In the movie *Dances with Wolves*, Kicking Bird speaks to Lt. Dunbar: "I was just thinking that of all the trails in this life there is one that matters most. It is the trail of a true human being. I think you are on this trail and it is good to see." How did Kicking Bird come to this understanding? By watching how Dunbar treated people. Dunbar's kindness, honesty, generosity, and acceptance impressed Kicking Bird into thinking that Dunbar was on the trail of a true human being. Dignity is a direction, the trail of a true human being, uncomplicated by the diversions and distractions of idols and false gods. It is about having a pure motive and a pure heart. In spite of stumbling on the path, losing your way and getting tired, dignity dictates that you know who you are and the direction you are going with your life. There will always be idols and false gods in your path – the world's alternatives to what you know is truly important. Stay on the path. You will see goodness in people. You will see beauty all around you. You will see God.

I'm intentionally defining dignity as having an uncomplicated and uncompromising direction for your life, which also means having an increasingly focused intention on seeing the dignity of others. Traditionally, the notion of purity seemed to be about maintaining correct behavior. I think that's the wrong idea – or, at least, an incomplete idea. Recall from my previous chapters that human beings are an admixture of dirt and spirit. We will get dirty. We will make wrong decisions, we will have times of being selfish and competitive, and we will unintentionally hurt other people. When that happens, we will apologize, make amends, reflect on what happened to take us off the road, then dust ourselves off and get back on the path. There is always something more to learn as we move forward. While it may be impossible to always behave correctly, it is not impossible to learn lessons, to grow in our ability to care about people, and to see the dignity and value in others.

What did Jesus mean when he said that we are blessed when we have a pure heart, when we stay on the path of dignity and care for others, for then we will see God? I liken this idea to John O'Donohue's notion that we should walk the earth with reverence so beauty will trust us. Walking the earth with reverence means carefully and gratefully seeing all that is around you. It means taking time to stand still with a heart open to the beauty that God has created and, within that beauty, to experience golden moments of transcendence.

There is also ugliness in the world. There is pain and suffering and poverty. You cannot walk on the earth with an open heart and not see and feel the suffering that is all around you. To be a person who is truly open, it would be impossible to hide from this reality. You cannot reconcile the absurd disparity between the beauty and the ugliness around us. We live in a world that is not as it should be, as it was intended to be. We won't be able to fix this, but we can still be kind. We can do what we can do, in large or small ways, to help, to treat others with dignity.

Kathe and I were enjoying our vacation in Costa Rica. Driving through the amazing countryside, looking for the hotel where we planned to spend the night, we became hopelessly lost. Tools like GPS and ordinary maps hadn't helped us and after going in circles for a time, we stopped at a tiny family "restaurant." I put quotes around the word restaurant – there were two tables outside, an elderly woman at a stove, and her daughter who walked out to greet us. The language barrier didn't help, but we decided to sit for a while and order something to drink. Seeing the look of frustration and exhaustion on our faces, the elderly woman behind the stove graciously brought us two tacos of cooked papaya and a small amount of ground meat. This is kindness, this is dignity. Of our vacation in Costa Rica, I remember the astonishing beauty of the place, but I remember most the small taco shop by the side of the road and that simple act of kindness.

Being Old

As older people we confront daily the betrayal of aging. Our bodies don't work as well. We don't have the energy or vitality that we once had. Things are harder to do; opening the lid of a jar can be challenging. How can you not be depressed as a result? Unfortunately, becoming depressed can come easily to older people. Physicians may misdiagnose the variety of symptoms of depression in the elderly as simply the consequences of aging. Similarly, family members and friends may too easily shrug off an older person's lapses of memory, lack of motivation, and loss of vitality.

My wife was alarmed at how fast her 80-year-old mother was declining. Having been trained as a psychotherapist, Kathe recognized symptoms of depression – symptoms that others, even her mother's physician, had missed. Her mom said that it was okay to talk with her doctor and Kathe suggested that he consider prescribing Mom an antidepressant. Wow! In a few weeks we couldn't believe the transformation. Mom was alive again – her old self had reemerged with more energy, more enthusiasm, and more humor. It was tempting to be angry at the doctor for dismissing Mom as an older person who was simply declining. But that anger would be misdirected. Anger, when controlled and focused, is energy for change. The energy of anger that we all felt at the doctor's passive acceptance of Mom's decline was redirected to making sure that she got the quality of care she needed to travel through the remaining journey of her life with dignity. She lived happily to the age of 94.

I think that this is what Dylan Thomas had in mind in his poem on aging, "Do Not Go Gentle Into That Good Night," where he famously tells us to rage against death. Just because you're old, the poem suggests, doesn't mean that you should give up the fight. Thomas encourages us to get angry. That isn't hard when you're fighting with the lid of a jar. But that isn't the right kind of anger. Again, anger, when controlled and focused, is energy for change. Of course, sometimes you feel like giving up - remember my chapter on "Why Bother?" My elderly client whose wife had died told me that he was not sure why he was still here. "There are times," he said, "when it's hard to get up in the morning, it's hard to face the day." I can certainly understand that. When living becomes a daily hassle, filled with frustrations and loss, it is hard to hold on to hope and hard to want to stay alive. What helps when we're old is our attitude.

Will Rogers, a legend in the early part of the 20th century, quipped that he "never met a man he didn't like." That seems pretty hard to believe - some people are pretty unlikeable. My guess is that Rogers wasn't talking about people, likable or unlikeable. Instead, he was revealing something about himself. I think he was talking about his attitude. He never met a man he didn't like because he chose not to dislike anyone.

Your attitude is among your most valuable resources as you age. Along with making sure that you have people in your life to talk to, be sure to have people in your life that you can care about. Your attitude should be less about what is missing in your life and more about not missing the reason why you are alive. Recall that dignity may be seen by how you treat others. Be constructively angry with yourself when you forget that bringing kindness to another that may make their day - may even save their life. It will certainly improve yours.

I've said that as we age, it feels like our body is betraying us. Why are our eyes weaker, our hearing weaker, our muscles weaker? We are living in a body that is up to no good and there's little we can do about it. Well, we can buy reading glasses, hearing aids, go for walks, and try to lift some weights, but we know where things are headed. Maybe that isn't so bad. Maybe slowing down isn't such a bad thing. It may be that as the outer world grows dimmer and harder to grasp, our inner life is becoming more present and maybe more interesting. That's a choice we have to make – or we could choose to watch television all day. That's not a terrible decision. You've earned the right to relax. Life takes its toll. It may be time to duck out of being responsible for everything and everyone. However, watching television all day gets old. It might also be a good idea to go outside for a walk, help out at church or with your family of faith, or find something else worthwhile to do. There are lots of other choices. And you can bring an attitude of dignity to all of your choices.

Life Choices

In an earlier chapter, I said that the most important choice we make as we age is whether or not to continue to live. By that, I don't mean merely surviving. You can stay in bed or in your easy chair. You may survive, but are you truly living? Perhaps you don't have a choice – age has taken its toll on your mobility. But if you decide to live, you'll find ways to engage with the world.

Our failing biology can feel like a betrayal or an invitation – we can choose. When it comes to choices, I think a reasonable first choice is to let someone know that you are lonely, if in fact you are. For many, that may be a difficult choice to make. People sometimes have trouble trusting other people. It isn't unusual for someone to think, "I don't want to be dependent on others – people have a way of disappointing, of letting you down. I've been hurt enough already. If I lean too heavily on a friend or family member, they will likely move away, or die, or get too busy to bother with me, and I'll be worse off than before." My response to that might be, "Yes, life is a gamble, and you may be hurt, but hurts can heal – loneliness doesn't heal unless you do something about it."

I wonder about the people who are lonely because they're embarrassed about how they look, or about being so frail, or are afraid of becoming a burden – they may feel like they've lost their dignity. I can understand that as well, and I have a solution: I hang out mostly with older people who are frail, who have lost the bloom of youth, don't remember things as well, and are self-conscious like me. That way we can all laugh and enjoy the companionship of other ditzy old-timers who pretty much all look alike. Notice that all-important word, "companionship." Being self-conscious doesn't help you to stay alive, but friends who care about you and are in the same boat can give you a reason to live. If they don't help you to stay healthy and live longer, they will, at least, help you find more of life to enjoy.

I hope you see that dignity isn't primarily about how you look to others, but how they look to you - I see my old-timer friends as dignified, no matter how many words they forget, or even if they're to the point of wearing diapers. Do you see the value in others? Is the direction you are taking and the choices you are making bringing kindness and compassion to the world? Mahatma Gandhi was one of the most respected men of all time. He didn't wear an expensive suit and a power tie; in fact, he wore his own home-spun cloth, and very little of that. He carried himself with dignity because he knew who he was and what he was offering to the world. You can do the same - you can walk the trail of your final years with grace and dignity.

"Though our outward man is decaying, yet our inward
man is renewed day by day."
2nd Cor. 4:16

CHAPTER 12

———————— • ————————

GUILT, SHAME, AND SORROW

Give sorrow words: the grief that does not speak
Whispers the o'er-fraught heart, and bids it break.

~William Shakespeare

In the journey of your life, you will pass through times of sorrow. You can't avoid it. Even if sorrow hasn't yet touched you directly, it is all around you. If your eyes are open you will see it and feel it. There's a saying, "You can't run away from trouble, ain't no place that far." The best thing to do is take Shakespeare's advice and give sorrow words. Find someone you trust and talk to them. There's another saying, "Confession is good for the soul." That exact saying doesn't occur in Christian scripture, although there are many references to the benefits of confessing sorrow or wrongdoing. The fact is that confession *is* good for the soul. Science has proven it.

I previously explained the relationship between one's spirit (transcendent values) and one's biology (what's required to sustain life). Soul is the relationship between the two. Since your soul is the connection between your spiritual life and your biological life, you don't want to clog up your soul with unresolved guilt, shame, or sorrow - it will make it harder to listen to your spirit as well as take care of your body. I'll explain.

Telling Your Story

As you tell your story, you will activate your memory, calling to mind images, physical sensations, and emotions. Memory may also trigger certain behavioral responses. A loud bang, for example, may send a soldier with Post-Traumatic Stress Disorder ducking for cover. The best therapy for war veterans and other survivors of trauma is to talk about what happened. Even though talking about it can be nearly as traumatic as the experience itself, it has to happen for the brain to heal. Brains heal through the process of neural integration. As a story of trauma unfolds, memories are activated. When someone is willing to continue the story and has the courage to access the horrible memories and emotions, the brain will distribute those emotions into other parts of the brain, lessening the intensity of the memories and emotions. People in recovery understand how difficult this is and will often repeat the saying, "You survived the trauma, you can survive the healing."

My wife asked a Vietnam veteran if he had ever talked about what happened to him in Vietnam. When he replied "No," my wife said, "You can tell me." Weeks went by and the horror and trauma of that war were eventually purged from his soul. Talk is good medicine. The authors of *A General Theory of Love* have this to say:

> The mind-body clash has disguised the truth that psychotherapy is physiology. When a person starts therapy, he isn't beginning a pale conversation; he is stepping into a somatic state of relatedness. Evolution has sculpted mammals into their present form - they become attuned to one another's evocative signals and alter the structure of one another's nervous systems. Psychotherapy's transformative power comes from engaging and directing these ancient mechanisms. Therapy is a living embodiment of limbic process as corporeal as digestion

or respiration. Without the psychologic unity limbic operations provide, therapy would indeed be the vapid banter some people suppose it to be.

Psychotherapy *is* physiology. Talk *is* medicine. According to Shakespeare, giving sorrow words will prevent a heart from breaking. But you don't need to visit a psychotherapist to enjoy the medicinal benefits of talk therapy. Find someone you trust and talk about what's bothering you. There are many sayings about the process of "getting things off your chest," such as "owning up," "making a clean breast," "bringing it out in the open," and "spilling it." People have known forever that talking about what's bothering you helps you to feel better even when they didn't understand how the brain does its healing work.

Guilt and Shame

The word "guilt" is typically used to describe the emotion that results from having behaved badly, whereas "shame" is used to describe how you feel about yourself as a result. So, guilt refers to *conduct* and shame refers to *character*. Both shame and guilt have positive and negative sides. If you take something that doesn't belong to you, feeling guilty will prompt you to return or pay for the item – that's the positive side. Feeling guilty years later because of a hurt that you caused, even if you've done everything you could do to rectify the situation, is the negative side of guilt. Living a lifetime feeling guilty will injure both your soul and your body. And it may be that the guilt you have felt turns into a lingering sense of shame.

Unfortunately, many dysfunctional family systems rely too heavily on guilt and shame to provide the emotional cohesion that rigidly regulates every aspect of family life. In these families, shame is felt not just for behaving *inappropriately* but for behaving *independently*. Shame researcher Dr. Brené Brown believes people can experience shame as an "unwanted identity." Growing up in a shame-based family may do more than simply regulate behavior; it may brand a person's identity. In therapy, I've heard people say, "I hate myself." This is the tragic consequence of growing up in a family where you were made to feel shame about *who* you are, not just *how* you behaved. Every thought and emotion carries the burden of self-judgment and self-rejection. The lingering consequences of this toxic shame are what cause many people to seek relief through drugs and alcohol, and may lead to an early death.

I had attention-deficit disorder growing up. I was often forgetful and disorganized. 60-plus years later, when my wife asks, "Did you forget?" I feel a twinge of shame. Thank goodness she is patient and forgiving. Over the years she has helped to heal many of my shame triggers. In his book, *Healing the Shame That Binds You* (1990), John Bradshaw describes "toxic" shame as more than just the feeling of *doing* something bad, but about the feelings of *being* bad. He describes family systems in which family members are taught to feel shame for being different, for not following the family norms or expectations. This type of toxic shame is among the most common and, unfortunately, among the most difficult emotions to heal. When shame has been internalized at a young age, it does more than effectively regulate behavior – it may kill, and definitely maim, a child's spirit. When shame insidiously permeates one's being and becomes woven into the psyche, the results may be lethal. "Breathing in" the atmosphere permeating a toxic family system can, over time, expose a person to shame and anxiety such that their body is affected. The net consequence is that a person carries the sometimes subtle, sometimes intense, feelings of shame deep within their core self.

Getting Stuck in a Bad Story

Living with shame or guilt erodes the soul. As a result, the vibrant life of a child may gradually turn to self-condemnation and self-victimization. Because children depend on parents for an understanding of themselves and a definition of the world around them, they are vulnerable to a damaged self-image. Dan Siegel discusses this in his 1999 book, *The Developing Mind:*

Therefore, caregivers are the architects of the way in which experience influences the unfolding of genetically preprogrammed but experience dependent brain development. Genetic potential is expressed within the setting of social experiences which directly influence how neurons connect to one another. Human connections create neuronal connections.

Science has demonstrated that the nature of early childhood attachments may set the stage for ongoing life challenges. In *The Stories We Are* (1995), Dan McAdams uses literary themes to amplify the importance of understanding how the nature of early childhood attachments affects the trajectory of a person's life:

Secure attachments may nudge us in the direction of comedy and romance, insecure attachment in the direction of tragedy and irony. By the time each of us reaches adolescence and adulthood, we are ready to create stories of a certain quality or type. By the time we think seriously about the meaning of our own lives, we may already be predisposed to create that meaning through the filtering glass of tragedy, comedy, irony, or romance.

It's tragic for a child to become stuck in a bad story, a story filled with little self-confidence, little self-esteem, and devoid of love. It would be even more tragic for a child to grow up feeling like a victim without acceptance and without hope, to be stuck in a victim's story of shame and self-pity. It would be hard for that child to see beyond an earlier story, to create a different story where he or she isn't a victim but, instead, a survivor or even a hero. If this has been your experience, you're not alone, but there are many other stories of people who have overcome terrible experiences from their past and found the ability to create a new story for themselves.

A Transfusion of Hope

Living daily with shame, guilt, or sorrow will eat away at your mental health and your physical resilience. It isn't hard to become depressed. Depression happens when life wears you down, when you're dealing with loss, or when your physiology isn't working properly. It's dangerous if your depression turns into despair. Don't let that happen; see a doctor to find out what's going on and whether you need medication. Too many older people think that just because they're older, it's natural to become depressed at times. Yes, at times, but if your depression is ongoing, you need to find out what's going on. It may be that you need to find a good friend, your pastor, or a therapist to talk to. The truth is that you shouldn't try to white-knuckle through a depression. Talk with your doctor and think about the best way to get a transfusion of hope. The Bible states, "Hope deferred makes the heart sick, but a desire fulfilled is a tree of life" (Proverbs 13:12).

Where can you go to get a transfusion of hope? I can tell you what works for me but you need to find out what works for you - is it being with friends or family, is it being in nature, is it listening to music or doing something creative, is it finding strength from a community of faith?

Despair and depression will steal your vitality and joy, especially if you harbor feelings of shame, guilt, or sorrow. Get rid of those thieves. Forgive yourself, forgive those who have hurt you, and find, as the proverb encourages, a desire, a direction, a creative pursuit, and a source of meaning. Find sources of hope. Find gratitude. Look for sources of joy - they are all around you.

John Muir grew up hiking the hills of Scotland and brought his love of nature to the wilds of North America. Perhaps his greatest contribution was significantly influencing the creation of Yosemite National Park. According to the naturalist author John Tallmadge, Muir would suffer "times of anguish." Of course he did - how could he not be affected by the ravages of loggers in Sequoia or the encroachment of civilization into his home in the mountains? To purge his anguish, Muir would spend weeks tramping the Sierra Nevada mountains with meager rations, his overcoat, and a copy of Emerson. It worked. The transcendental writings of Emerson and the rugged beauty of the mountains kept Muir sane. The mountain air was a tonic to his soul. He lived a story worth remembering and celebrating, a story that reminds us that when we look for it, we can find reasons to live. He wrote, "Climb the mountains and get their good tidings. Nature's peace will flow into you as sunshine flows into trees. The winds will blow their own freshness into you, and the storms their energy, while cares will drop away from you like the leaves of autumn."

On this leg of your final journey, do whatever it takes – start therapy, talk with trusted friends and advisors, join an uplifting community, consider medications, pursue whatever is tonic to your soul – in order to enter the afterlife unencumbered by the thieves of shame, guilt, and sorrow.

CHAPTER 13

———————— ● ————————

WHEN THE JOURNEY IS HARD – JOB, SUFFERING, AND ROCKS IN THE ROAD

At this, Job got up and tore his robe and shaved his head. Then he fell to the ground in worship.

~Job 1:20

The Biblical story of Job offers much wisdom for the difficult parts of our final journey (and there will be difficult parts). It doesn't matter if you consider The Book of Job to be a sacred text or a powerful myth, or if you substitute "creator" or "the universe" or "spirit" or your "higher power" for God in this chapter - regardless, we can all learn from this story about what happens on our journeys when the road gets rough and there are obstacles before us that seem insurmountable.

In the Old Testament of the Bible, Job is a wealthy man known for his piety and faith in God. When Satan taunts God, insisting Job's faith would collapse if he was tested, God takes away Job's children, his wealth, and his livelihood in a single day, yet Job refuses to curse and renunciate God. I imagine Job looking at his razor - looking at it long and hard - looking at it wistfully. The Oxford Dictionary describes wistfully as: "a feeling of vague or regretful longing." I think that's the right word. How much easier it might be to take the razor to his throat. He must have felt the onslaught of the terrible suffering to come. Can you imagine losing all of that in a single day? Perhaps you can. Accidents, tornados, war, acts of violence, and death can do that. Most of the rest of us cannot begin to imagine what that could possibly feel like.

Job looked at his razor. I imagine he looked at it long and hard and longingly. Yet the torment was not over. Satan taunted God a second time, insisting that Job's faith would collapse if his body was also attacked. So Job was afflicted with sores. The medical community has different ideas about what that might have been. One source suspects that it was a form of leprosy. Job had to continually scrape away the dead and draining skin from this loathsome infliction. A Hebrew translation of the word "sores" is boils, an unrelenting, burning, skin disease that tormented Job night and day.

Curse God and Die

The Bible tells us almost nothing about Job's wife, but she's known for these words she spoke to him: "Curse God and die." Was she, as some have written, an instrument of Satan to push Job to the brink, encouraging him to suicide? Did she think that his steadfastness was cowardness, the way he passively accepted his fate? She must have said this in exasperation, in exhaustion, and in the hopelessness of her own suffering – after all, she lost her children, her livelihood, her wealth, her future, and her husband as she had known him. Maybe she was at the end of her own emotional rope. Or maybe she said this out of compassion for a husband who was suffering terribly, in a desire that he be released. Scripture doesn't say, so we can only speculate.

However she said what she said, and however she meant it, it was not comforting for Job. How hard it is to hold onto hope when the person nearest to you has given up hope. Job probably understood his wife's emotional surrender. His response to her doesn't seem to be especially harsh. "You are talking like a foolish woman. Shall we accept good from God, and not trouble?" This reminder from Job to his wife is the key to understanding the Book of Job and the key to understanding how Job was able to endure his many tortures.

Shall We Accept Good from God and Not Trouble?

In Chapter 5, I discussed the difference between faith *for* and faith *in*. Job's faith was grounded in his deep knowledge of the nature of God. It was clearly faith *in*. Added to his question above is this startling counterintuitive confession: "Though he slay me, yet will I trust him." Again, this comes from Job's deep understanding of the nature of God, a God that can be trusted even in the worst of life's calamities and abuses. How do you get that kind of faith? Is it blind optimism or wishful thinking or something else entirely?

The key to understanding the Book of Job is to understand the "subject-object" relationship between human beings and their creator. Scientific rigor insists that the nature of the object to be investigated determines the methodology of its investigation. Consequently, you use a microscope to study amoebas and a telescope to study the heavens. What do you use to study God?

Microscopes and telescopes are useful for studying His creation. Scripture is useful for knowing His thoughts, His nature, and His will. Yet, what about Who He is in Himself? That can only happen by having a relationship with Him. God sees your heart. He is less interested in your character than in your desires. In fact, your character can be defined *by* your desires. What do you want? What do you desire? Do you want to be a good person? Good. Do you want God, or your higher power, as a companion on your journey? Better. Do you want to be on His journey? Best of all. God knows this about people. The people worth remembering who have been on hard journeys are those who have been on His journey, the work He is doing in the world. What do you want for the rest of your journey?

What did Job Want?

I don't think that Job's focus was simply on being a good person. I think his focus, his appetite, was to know God. John Calvin said that we have no true knowledge of ourselves without first knowing God. If, like Job, your desire is to know God, you are better able to know yourself. In fact, you are bound to be horrified by what the tragedy that would result from running away from Him, like Satan did. Narcissistic pride is one result. God asked Satan what he had been up to. Satan replied, in effect, whatever I want - roaming throughout the earth, going back and forth on it. He must have thought that the earth belonged to him. (Actually, because of mankind's betrayal of God, it does. However, that's a different book.) Satan was gripped by narcissistic pride - the source of all sin.

Scripture doesn't tell us what motivated Job to have a heart fixed on knowing God. I wish it had. I wish I knew. However, if I did know then I might think that I was the subject of the work and the knowledge, and not one who is blessed with God's gift of insight and inspiration. The apostle Paul, writing to a church in Philippi, Greece, said that you work out your own "salvation," - a right relationship with God - when you know Who is in charge, Who is doing the deeper work. Job must have known Who was in charge: "Shall we only accept good from God...?" This faith is "righteousness."

How Do You Get It Right?

You get it right when you know, for sure, that you are the object and not the subject of your relationship with God. We do not predicate God. God predicates us. We know God by paying close attention to His own self-disclosure in the Bible and in the hearts of those who diligently seek Him. David got it right when he proclaimed, "The *Lord* is my shepherd." Others have gotten it right through the centuries. Do a search looking for people whose heart was right toward God. I trust it will be an inspiring project.

Job is a complex character. He certainly had doubts and questions. Yet, I think he did get it right: "I know that my redeemer lives, and that in the end he will stand on the earth. After my skin has been destroyed, yet in my flesh I will see God; I myself will see him with my own eye - I, and not another. How my heart yearns within me!" That last sentence is the key. Job had been through the harrowing mill. Recall that a mill is used for grinding. Job's encounter with God ground him into flour - flour that God would use to mold and bake and nurture all of us who are trying to get it right - those of us who are going through our own individual trials.

Job put down the razor and walked into Satan's grinding mill. Did he know what he was doing? I think he knew God. I think he trusted Him. I don't think he could have known the outcome. I don't think it mattered. Through it all he exclaimed, confidently, that he knew he would see God. Toward the last, he said, "My ears had heard of you but now my eyes have seen you." Is there anything in life more valuable than that? How do you get it right? God gives us the answer through His prophet Jeremiah: "You shall seek me and find me when you search for me with your whole heart."

When You're Suffering on Your Journey

When you're suffering, you already know that you need someone to talk to, perhaps a support group or community of faith. You know that you need to hold on to hope and try to have some perspective. You know to try your best to find something to be grateful for and to surround yourself with things or places that minister beauty. Here are some other ideas:

Write an exceptionally honest letter about how you're feeling. Address it to God or to someone that you trust won't judge your feelings.

- Keep a journal as did C.S. Lewis. Call it a pain journal, or a gratitude journal.
- Find someone else to help and care about.

- Examine yourself. Are you suffering more than you need to because of some notion of fairness or just desserts?
- Pray daily, even if it feels rote. Soon it will begin to feel genuinely authentic.

Rocks in the Road

There are no easy paths through life, paths without ruts, rocks, and ravines, and sometimes chasms. At a minimum, there will be the small rocks - pebbles that annoy you, loose rocks that may cause you to trip, and the occasional boulder that you will have to detour around. There is no easy path through life and a wise person learns not to pretend that life is either easy or fair but learns, instead, to anticipate difficulties and discover the best ways to move forward.

The Rock of Fairness

The concept of fairness is a rock upon which you can build the solid structure of your life. The concept of fairness underpins moral and ethical behavior with directives to "do unto others, as you would have them do unto you," and "love others as you love yourself." Endeavor, always, to treat everyone including yourself fairly. Make fairness a hallmark of your character.

However, if you look to others and to life to be fair in return, you will be constantly disappointed. In addition, if you try too hard to expect or enforce the idea of fairness on others, you will become a very angry person. The idea that life *should* be fair is a different kind of rock - it's actually a boulder on your path. Curse it if you wish. It isn't going anywhere, nor is your course. If you refuse to come to grips with the myth of life's fairness, you will stay stuck behind that boulder. How many people will be still stuck there along with you? You may have to make the choice that Job made to rend your garments, cry out in despair, and give up on the idea of fairness. The final word in the universe is not fairness. It is grace!

Blessings from Boulders

I could tell you so many stories about how people have had to face huge challenges. Sometimes, those challenges were insurmountable and became sources of strength. Sometimes, they found their way around the boulder and were able to discover a new path (perhaps the one less traveled).

There is a story in the New Testament about the Apostle Paul suffering with "a thorn in the flesh." Some called this thorn a type of physical pain or disability. Paul said that it was a messenger from Satan to torment him. Either way, he prayed to God to help him get rid of it. God's reply is interesting. "My grace is sufficient for you." What do you think that means?

I think that Job knew what it meant. My guess is that God knew Paul as well as He knew Job and reassured Paul that he already had what he needed – not for suffering to end, but to accept it with grace. Moreover, Paul's thorn, in God's mind, would only strengthen him – polishing his soul.

What quality did Paul and Job have that would buffer them against formidable pain, suffering, and loss? I think they had what most of us struggle with: complete confidence in the *nature* of God. However, I don't imagine that they had complete confidence in what God had in store for them. When Shadrach, Meshach, and Abednego faced the wrath of King Nebuchadnezzar for not worshiping his image and were condemned to burn in a furnace, they couldn't predict the outcome. Yet, they somehow saw beyond their immediate peril and announced that they would not bow down. They confidently proclaimed that God would deliver them, but "even if He doesn't," they would not bow down. This is, in effect, what Job said: "Though He slay me, yet will I trust Him." This is what David said: "Even though I may walk through the valley of the shadow of death, You will be with me. Your rod and staff will comfort me." This is what the apostle Paul said: "Therefore I will rejoice in my tribulation," understanding that he would find strength in the midst of it. Somehow, this is what we must also learn to say: I know who You are. I know Your grace and wisdom. Whatever is on my path You will be with me.

The Rock of Forgiveness

Like the rock of fairness, the rock of forgiveness is a rock upon which you can build a solid foundation of character. The ability to be a gracious and forgiving person is grounded in a strong commitment to maintaining a subject-object relationship with your creator. You are not the author but the object of His grace and forgiveness. The essence of forgiveness is transferring judgment to Him. He knows everything. You don't.

It is exceptionally difficult to forgive at times. I'm sure you may recall someone in your life who was particularly difficult for you to forgive. Probably everyone has. There have been people throughout history who many imagine would certainly not qualify to be forgiven for their narcissistic atrocities. Again, understand that forgiveness isn't merely emotional work and even less a work of letting someone off the hook. I said this in Chapter 1 and it bears repeating: forgiveness is an act of your will to transfer judgment to God. Importantly, it is releasing yourself from the burden of judgment. Surely God will judge correctly. The Bible says, wisely, "Judge not, lest ye be judged."

If you cannot let go of anger and resentment, if you hold on to the hurt, the unfairness, the emotional memory of having been wounded, there will be a boulder in your path that will not move and you will not be able to detour around. You've heard this before, and it's true: forgiving someone is not only for their benefit but for yours. You don't want to stay stuck behind the boulder of unforgiveness; it will cripple your soul.

The Rock of Freedom

God spoke creation into existence but spoke directly *to* human beings. This fact, more than any other, defines what it is to be a human being. Humans have "response-ability." We have been endowed by our creator with life and liberty, and we are responsible to respond with the best of our abilities. How will we use this freedom?

A responsible person is a person who chooses to care, who chooses to be responsive to God, to others, to the planet. This choosing is a rock upon which we are able to build a life that has true value. We have heard that with freedom comes responsibility. Of course it does. What good use can be made of freedom without being responsible with it? Understandably, human beings make increasingly better choices with their freedom and responsibility as they mature. In Ken Wilber's theories of the stages of spiritual development, he states that when we are infants, we feel responsible only for ourselves and our own needs. As we mature, our concern for others extends to our family members, our sports team, tribe, and nation. When we are fully mature, we know that we cannot isolate ourselves from the rest of the world or abuse our planet. We broaden out the spheres of our responsibility. Our spiritual development has evolved, from *me*, to those *close to us*, and then to *all of us*.

If you choose to remain an infant, concerned only with your own needs and well-being, or if you choose to remain an adolescent, over-invested in your team crushing the competition, your political party winning, and your country prospering at the expense of other nations, your freedom is a huge boulder on your path. You stay stuck behind it. How many others are stuck there with you, refusing to mature as human beings?

The story of Job contains wisdom for us at the end of our life's journey. We will most likely not be exempt from suffering, and we may experience life as unfair, but we can remain faithful, knowing we are still graced by the love of our creator. We can practice forgiveness, we can embrace our response-ability, and we can accept the gift of freedom.

CHAPTER 14

RETIREMENT

An elegant sufficiency, content,
Retirement, rural quiet, friendship, books

~James Thomson

I have a great dentist – the same one I've had for close to thirty years. So, I was a little nervous when he said recently that he was thinking about retirement. "Don't worry," he reassured me, "it's a ways off." He wondered out loud how to think about it, how to fill his time, how to find a new source of identity. He also wondered how his retirement would affect his marriage. I didn't have much to say as I waited for the local anesthetic to take effect. I simply thanked him for an idea for my book, realizing that I had overlooked the very essential topic of retirement. As I began to think about how to think about the challenges of retirement, I came up with five subtitles. I had to alliterate them so my brain could retain them while the dentist was working. I came up with the topic headings of choice, challenge, community, contribution, and contentment. I also thanked God for the invention of anesthetics.

This chapter is primarily focused on offering advice as you're considering retirement. Don't worry – if you've already retired, there'll still words of wisdom here for living most fully during your retirement years.

To Live or Die

The most important decision to make when you retire is do you want to continue to live, and if you do want to live, how do you plan to keep yourself alive? Those may seem like simple choices, but you might be surprised at how many of us are lazy about thinking productively about how to keep ourselves alive. Once you step off the conveyor belt of obligations, you typically face many new challenges.

The choice to stay alive won't get you far if it's easy and automatic and not made with care and true determination that your life matters and is worth holding on to. The choice to stay alive must be *intentional*. The second part of that choice is choosing what you need to do to *keep* yourself alive. Those will be choices that you will make every day – good or bad choices about taking care of yourself. Now that we're older it seems easier to avoid the hard choices like daily exercise, staying on a food plan, being less sedentary, contacting a friend, and being more involved or active. Those are life-affirming choices. The alternative may be spending the day binge-watching television.

What's wrong with watching television? What's wrong with spending a few days a week playing golf, or gardening, or doing nothing at all? "I'm retired," you argue. "I've worked hard all my life. Don't I deserve to do whatever I feel like?" The answer is yes and no. Of course you deserve to relax and do things you enjoy, or not do much of anything. But, if you've made a consciously determined decision to stay alive, you will want to add a few more things to the list. I think in terms of energy *in* and energy *out*. Energy in requires more than halting the outflow of energy out (although that helps). Energy *in* is finding activities that are renewing and revitalizing, activities that provide a nutritious source of life energy and vitality.

In the saying above, James Thomson made his list. He was a Scottish poet who lived in the early part of the 18th century. He had some good ideas – although spending the day reading books might not be everyone's cup of tea – his focus seemed to be on living a quiet life in retirement. My goodness, so many people who have worked hard in their lives would certainly agree. While that may be the ideal for many retirees today, be careful that you don't overdue your vegetative transformation while you're still among us. It may also be good to find some things to challenge your mind and heart to enable you to continue to live while you're alive.

Challenges

Throughout this book, I've quoted our current surgeon general Dr. Vivek Murthy who said that human beings are "hardwired for connection." I think we are also hardwired for growth. From a young age, we have wanted to grow, not just physically but psychologically and relationally. These, in addition to growing in our various competencies. We pushed ourselves to learn new skills, competed to perfect competencies, and stretched to acquire abilities. We liked feeling competent and competitive. We had a variety of motives. We wanted to be more sexually attractive, we wanted admiration, we wanted to prepare ourselves for our life and our life's work, or we simply wanted to have fun. However, tragically, many people are motivated simply by the need to survive.

What about now? You've solved most of life's problems and answered most of life's questions. You know who your life's partner is - or was. You know whether or not you'll have children. You know where you're going to live and how you will earn money. You made a living, survived setbacks, and developed relationships. You answered these questions and most of these challenges are behind you.

It's true that for some of you, your challenge is that you won't be able to retire in the classic sense. You'll simply hope to continue to have enough money to live. This may be the only challenge you can afford. However, if you're fortunate enough not to have to worry about keeping body and soul together, then you face other challenges. What may be your main challenge? Is it boredom, illness, depression, staying healthy, getting along with people, finding meaning? Welcome to old age. Gilda Radner of *Saturday Night Live* and my wise mother both used to say, "If isn't one thing, it's another." For some, it's all of the above. Yes, aging requires facing challenges with courage.

If your choice is to live, then you have two options in facing these challenges: live with them or deal with them. You can surrender and go gently into the good night, as Dylan Thomas warned, or rage against that same night. If you don't feel up to *raging,* how about simply *resolving*? Resolve to discover contexts for kindness. Look around you. People are in desperate need of kindness. Your soul is nurtured by kindness as well as being kind to others.

Above, I listed some of the challenges we face as we age. If you're bored, it could be because you've decided not to deal with these challenges. It may follow that illness, depression, loneliness, and not getting along with people may be the result. It seems that Dylan Thomas' father had given up on life and was waiting for death. Critics think that Thomas, in his poem, was expressing his own grief and trying to get his father to be less passive about going gently into his death.

Certainly, there comes a time when it is appropriate to accept the fact that you are near the end of your journey. In fact, that acceptance will make it more likely that you will have the important, albeit bittersweet, conversations with your family and friends that you need to have in saying your goodbyes. Yet, how will you know when to rage and when to relax? I don't know how you'll know. I don't know how I'll know. I don't plan to rage, but I do plan to hold on to life as long as I can.

Community

I've already written an entire chapter on the importance of community (Chapter 9). I'll simply reiterate that we need people to talk to, people to care about, people to care about us, and people to support us when we need it. Recall what Dr. Vivek Murthy, in his book *Together*, warned about the dangers of isolation: loneliness, increased stress, depression, hopelessness, despair, and eroding health.

Some people prefer isolation. They hate the feeling of being dependent. They will try to live by themselves and manage the best they can - until they can't. Good for them. It's good to feel independent as long as possible; but beware of the potential consequences of isolation that Dr. Murthy listed. Preferring not to be dependent is one thing but hiding out from people because you're embarrassed about having a failing body, or not wanting to burden your family, or having feelings of social anxiety, can be dangerous.

Speaking of community, if you have a spouse who's still alive, are they ready for you to retire? Better find out. That may be a difficult conversation, but one you both need to have. When one or both of you retire, there will be momentous changes and challenges for your relationship. Among other things, you will have to renegotiate some of the rules of your relationship. Oh, and all relationships have rules. Some relationship rules are obvious about dos and don'ts, and some are less obvious or simply understood. An interesting conversation to have with your spouse is to explore these overt and covert relationship rules. You live with those rules - you might as well be conscious enough of their existence to make sure they're either working for you, or they need to be renegotiated or replaced. It would be good for each of you to make a list and come to the negotiating table with an open mind and heart. On the other hand, some negotiations are ongoing and need to be visited again and again, and perhaps, again.

Couples negotiate finances, household chores, entertainment, various values, their romantic relationship, faith practices and - here's the big one - time together and time apart. If there were children in the home, there wasn't much available time to negotiate. If you and your spouse were both employed - same thing. Everything's different now and open to re-negotiation. Do you have your financial plans worked out? Do you have similar appetites for time spent socializing and seeing family? Be sure to keep your romance alive, even if it's simply occasional dinners out, extra hugs, and plenty of "love yous!" What may be more difficult to navigate, now that you are not employed outside of the home and the kids are not underfoot, is your time together and your time apart.

For some of you, this will be less difficult. You already have well-established hobbies, pastimes, and routines that provide an adequate amount of that all-important alone time and time with friends. Even if you are best friends with your spouse, you love hanging out together, and you enjoy similar activities, it's essential that you plan to give each other an adequate amount of space. There's such a thing as being too close.

Why is being "too close" a potential problem? The quick answer is that you'll get on each other's nerves. Little irritations and inconveniences can be tolerated. However, when you're dancing together in a small space, you have to watch out for toes. People have different ways of enjoying dancing. Some like a slower pace and others are more exuberant. Like marriage, you can negotiate your dance styles for a short while but before long it may turn into a power struggle. Best to take a break and not continually try to make something work that doesn't. Find a routine that gives you adequate time together and an adequate time apart. Be willing to be flexible with your routine. It makes dancing together more fun.

My widowed client tells me that he doesn't know how to be in his huge house now that he's the only one there. He said that when his wife was alive, they each had their own space in the same house to retreat to. That works. It's easier when you have room enough to avoid stepping on each other's toes. But if you live in an apartment or small house, someone has to find a way to exit on occasion. Giving each other space – balancing time together and time apart – is vital for your relationship to last, even when you like each other.

This is where the all-important conversations must happen. Be realistic and honest about your appetite for both connection and independence. It may be a difficult, perhaps painful, conversation, but find a compromise that works and make the deal. You may have a partner who thinks that if people really love each other, they should want to spend all of their time together. It doesn't work. People need time together and time apart – time to think their own thoughts, pursue their individual interests and creative projects, or just not have to worry, for a time, about the other person. We all need time by ourselves.

Practicing psychotherapists are not ethically permitted to have a dual relationship where they have a relative, friend, or business partner as a client. So I couldn't charge my father when he asked me for advice.

"How do I deal with your mother?" Dad asked. "Now that we are both retired, she wants to spend all of our time together and won't even let me go to the store by myself." I was tempted to respond, "Dad, good luck with that." But I thought of a better response: "Dad, I think you need to be honest with Mom. She's wise enough for you to simply explain that you need time to do some things on your own. It may sting a bit but she can handle it and you don't want to accrue resentments." It worked. Later Dad told me that Mom understood and appreciated his honesty.

Contribution

Your life is valuable. Perhaps you have already made significant contributions. You have supported a family, raised children, loved and cared about people, and made a difference in your community or in your place of worship. Maybe you have been kind to others. Maybe you have created something that will last. Maybe what will last is what people will say about you. What do you think? Is there more left to do?

Of course, there's always more left to do. You're still alive. You've made the choice to be alive. You will live even longer, if you want to, by finding meaningful work to invest yourself in. There is plenty of meaningful work to be done. Retirement isn't about the freedom to do nothing, as some people may suppose. Retirement is about the freedom to find something important to live for, something that will make a difference, something that is worth staying alive for. You are now an elder and what do elders do? Among other things, and maybe the most important thing, is to tell stories.

Be sure to tell stories. This is one of the most valuable contributions you can make. Tell stories to your children and grandchildren. If they'll listen, tell stories to your friends. Somebody once said that a true friend is someone who will listen to you and someone who will tell you the truth. It's important to have those kinds of friends. It's important to have someone in your life who is both interested and interesting. There is something very therapeutic about talking about your life, your experiences and your memories, and it's especially therapeutic if you have someone who is genuinely interested in you. It helps to put some things in perspective and share important events and memories. Why is that?

You may recall from an earlier chapter that I discussed the healing potential in accessing the emotions that live inside a given story. Recall that "neural integration" is the brain's ability to metabolize emotion, lessening the pain inside memories of past hurts. In addition to the process of neural integration, telling stories helps you to feel feelings. Catharsis is kind of cleaning out of the cobwebs inside of the emotional "rooms" that have been closed up for years.

This isn't a new idea. Since ancient times people have been getting things off their chest, confessing and unburdening themselves of the memory of painful experiences or guilty self-betrayal. Retirement should be a welcome time for reflection and perhaps confession. It will be hard for you to find a member of the clergy who hasn't heard your story repeated many times in one form or another. Without the professional anonymity of a priest, rabbi, or imam, it may be harder to trust a good friend with unflattering information about yourself and your life. Try it and find out. Find out if your friend truly is your friend. And if your friend truly is your friend, you can share and celebrate your joys and triumphs as well. They won't have to pretend that the photos of your grandchildren aren't, in fact, absolutely adorable.

Contentment and Joy

Contentment isn't actually the right word for the fifth important thing to focus on in your retirement; but I was sitting in a dentist chair thinking about what to write and having to alliterate my bullet points in my head so I could remember them. A better word for what I have in mind is "enjoyment" – finding joy. Where do you look for joy? This is truly an important question. If you are looking for joy and if your heart is open, joy will find you. Joy is elusive. You can't orchestrate it like you can happiness. Happiness is about something happening, something that makes you smile, something you can buy or do or make. Joy is different. This is what the Oxford scholar, C.S. Lewis, said about joy in his 1955 book, *Surprised by Joy*:

> I call it Joy, which is here a technical term and must be sharply distinguished both from Happiness and Pleasure. Joy (in my sense) has indeed one characteristic, and one only, in common with them; the fact that anyone who has experienced it will want it again.... I doubt whether anyone who has tasted it would ever, if both were in his power, exchange it for all the pleasures in the world. But then Joy is never in our power and Pleasure often is.

Joy will appear when it wants. There will be those golden moments when you look across the room at your family enjoying themselves, your grandchildren squabbling, your spouse laughing and, in that moment, you will well up with gratitude that you are alive, that you have been alive. If you have no family, spouse, or grandchildren, go to a park. Joy is there as well. Watch the exuberance of children, the tenderness of lovers, the happiness of someone playing with his dog. Look carefully. Life is precious and fleeting, but there is love here, and joy.

Recall what John O'Donohue said. "When you walk on the earth with reverence, beauty will decide to trust you." When you walk, open-hearted, the paths of a park, a garden, a quiet woodland, or the desert at night, you will know what the shepherd boy David from the Old Testament knew: "The heavens declare the glory of God."

The word "enjoyment" is overused and undervalued. You can enjoy a movie or a nice cup of coffee. Go deeper. To en-joy is to find the joy inside. This is what O'Donohue means by walking with reverence. It is walking intentionally, with a heart open to seeing the extraordinary ordinary, and being open to those golden moments of quietness and gratitude for the gift of life.

I'd like to conclude with a quote from Patrick O'Brien's about Captain Aubrey in the book *Treason's Harbor*: "He had a strong sense of his life being upon the turn, between two seasons, as it were, with the certainties of the one no longer valid for the other." You may have a similar sense of life being "upon the turn." Going into retirement can feel like that. On the one hand, the certainties of earlier years may no longer seem as valid. It may be hard to count on our bodies functioning as effectively as they once did. It may be easier to forget things or to find helpful excuses for delaying chores. Without the weekly routine of obligations, retirement can be both a blessing and a challenge, as well as both meaningful and enjoyable. Returning to my first point in this chapter, it's about choices. Each day of retirement presents choices to move toward life – toward health and joy as well as to the many opportunities to be kind, and each day of retirement can be a day to thank God for the gift of your life.

CHAPTER 15

WHAT DRAWS US TO WONDER

Here is another interesting point of interest and side trip on your journey. As I did with Atul Gawande's book *Being Mortal*, I will review the extraordinary research of Dr. Bruce Greyson into the phenomena of near-death experiences (NDEs) in his 2021 book, *After*. The book is fascinating to read and deserves its own chapter, because NDEs are more common than you think – Grayson's research says one in twenty Americans has experienced one, meaning we all probably know someone who has. The chapter, however, is a challenge for me to write as I consider myself a conservative Christian. I believe in the resurrection of Jesus Christ and the authority of the Old and New Testaments, including what scripture reports about the life hereafter. However, alongside my Christian beliefs, I was impressed by Greyson's scholarly research in this book, a compilation of 45 years of research into near-death experiences. The challenge for me is to hold my Christian faith in one hand and Greyson's exciting research in the other. I won't try to harmonize the two. I'll simply report the remarkable research from this remarkable researcher.

Greyson is careful not to come to any religious or metaphysical conclusions from his research, nor does he advocate the popular psychological explanation that the brain creates the mind and therefore NDEs are the result of brain functioning. As any good scientist, he simply reports his findings. He states that being intellectually honest requires avoiding taking sides in the debate between the idea that the brain creates NDEs and that NDEs occur outside of brain functioning. I appreciate Greyson's scientific objectivity. His findings make the adventure of discovery into what happens after death all the more intriguing and exciting.

The Mind is Not the Brain

One conclusion Greyson seems forced to consider is that the brain does not create the mind. This conclusion flies in the face of the traditional view that the mind is an extension of the brain. For example, I have tremendous respect for Antonio Damasio and his research into how the brain may create the conscious mind. In his 1999 book *The Feeling of What Happens: Body and Emotion in the Making of Consciousness,* Damasio provides a careful and convincing account of how consciousness arises from the "intelligent" interaction of each cell in our body.

Among the brain's multifunctional tasks is to monitor our interior biological processes – awareness of changes in our internal physical states as well as awareness of awareness. In short, this awareness of awareness creates consciousness. No problem so far. However, how does the brain create consciousness when the brain itself is dead? The challenge for science is to answer that question.

Greyson points out that in science, different tools are needed for different tasks. That the brain creates thoughts and feelings is a useful tool for understanding how the brain functions in everyday life; however, a different tool is needed to understand how the brain continues to create strikingly intense and vivid images and associations when the brain has been deprived of oxygen and fuel. Damasio's "tool" for explaining the creation of consciousness may not be the right tool to explain the experience of expanded consciousness when the brain is no longer involved. One would have to cross over a philosophical and epistemological bridge to find that tool.

Our brain has three principal tasks: maintaining our sanity, our security, and our significance. Of the three, *sanity* is clearly the top priority. In addition, the brain's investment in the survival of the organism means that it must be vigilant about our *security*. Being *significant* simply means securing and maintaining sufficient status among other mammals so that we continue to benefit from their help and protection, and not get eaten.

Again, sanity is job one. The brain has multifunctional safeguards for maintaining sanity. It "filters" out much of what we might be aware of in order to facilitate our grasp on the essential tasks in the here and now. Anxiety, for example, is an essential filtering emotion. The brain seems to create enough useful anxiety necessary to pay attention to our present or future needs and circumstances. Too much anxiety, on the other hand, is debilitating for many people whose brains are disordered.

The existence of NDEs presents an interesting question regarding the connection between brain and mind. People who have had a near-death experience report a tremendous expansion of awareness. Without the brain's filtering effects, colors are brighter, sensations and sounds are heightened, and emotions are more intense. In addition, experiencers accurately report perceptions of things going on outside and around their bodies; for example, the conditions and the people in an operating theater while the patient is unconscious. How can this be possible unless the mind is freed from the limiting filter of the brain?

"Those paradoxes," Greyson states, "suggest that we need a different model of how minds and brains interact. They suggest that the physical brain may act like a cell phone, receiving thoughts and feelings from the nonphysical mind and converting them into electrical and chemical signals that the body can understand and use. And they suggest that – in extreme circumstances at least – minds can function quite well without brains to filter them."

Although I began this chapter with a confession that it has not been an easy chapter for me to write, I cannot imagine that any exploration of an afterlife would be easy. I think the challenge for afterlife explorers is to be cautious about bold assertations, given that no one knows for sure how to explain what they've experienced.

The Universal and Personal Aspects of NDEs

NDE experiencers report phenomena experienced similarly by others. At the same time, what is recalled by an individual is organized and filtered through the individual's brain. Those reporting NDEs characteristically have a difficult time condensing and describing these extraordinary experiences into intelligible language. In addition to the limitations of language, there must also be cultural influences on the reports that select words and images from within specific cultural contexts. This means that even if individuals report similar phenomena (universal), those phenomena may be interpreted and explained differently (personal).

Here are some of the similar experiences reported:

- Being outside or above one's body, floating, observing one's body from above
- Traveling swiftly, often with the sense of rapidly moving through a tunnel
- Inexpressible illumination, brilliant, penetrating light
- A profound sense of deep peace
- An awareness of unconditional love
- Seeing familiar people
- A rapid reviewing of one's life without feeling judged or condemned

This last item, a life review, has been described as a simultaneous awareness not only of an individual's actions but also of how these actions affected others. The effect of a life review is not judgment but increased awareness and empathy.

Judgment

Are people judged for their behaviors on earth? Christians think so. Jews think so. Muslims think so. Hinduism, Buddhism, and Jainism proffer the notion of karma. It seems that each of these world faiths believes in the idea of cosmic accountability. Why is that? It makes sense that people ought somehow to be rewarded for doing good and punished for doing bad. I suppose that comes from the idea of fairness and justice. I can easily come up with a list of people who many of us would agree were very bad people, acting unjustly, unfairly, and cruelly.

Still, I wonder if this is an intrinsic human value and belief that informs our faith and understanding of God and creation, or if our creator has endowed us with this value, expressed in different ways in different faiths? A cultural anthropologist might argue that the concept of justice has endured since the beginning of time. It just made good sense to early peoples to maintain certain social standards of behavior – so perhaps less nature than nurture. Thomas Jefferson, on the other hand, advocated for the nature side of the argument: "We hold these truths to be self-evident, that all men are created equal, that they are endowed by their Creator with certain unalienable Rights." These rights include the right to live, the right to freedom of choice, and the right to pursue happiness. Jefferson, writing a legal document, used the term "right," but I prefer the term "impulse" to shift the focus from what we are given legally to how we were created – our internal moral compass. I believe we have an impulse to live, an impulse toward freedom of choice, and an impulse to pursue happiness.

Because of this, I'll go with both nature and nurture. I think that Thomas Jefferson was right that we are endowed with certain rights and impulses to want to live, to choose freely, and to be able to pursue happiness. And anthropologists are also right – from our early history, human beings have developed norms of social conduct. These norms/laws have been inscribed in clay, painted on walls, and printed on paper. The U.S. Constitution does what it can to explicate and enforce those norms/laws.

What is justice? Here the conversation becomes really interesting. Justice is a wrestling match between grace and truth. Some would prefer using the word compassion instead of grace. A man steals bread to feed his starving children. He is a thief, breaking the law. It follows, according to laws enacted by human beings at various times and in various cultures, that his punishment might be to lose his hand as punishment. If he were shown compassion, would the thief and society be sufficiently deterred against theft? If one were prone toward compassion, what would be the justification and how would compassion be enacted in a way that does not injure truth? This is what I mean by a wrestling match.

It seems that all faith practices believe in a benevolent and merciful creator who judges compassionately. I hope they're right. I can't speak for what other faiths believe about the nature and consequences of justice and judgment. I can't even speak exhaustively about the nature of judgment in the Christian faith, with its many diverse sects. The problem and promise of the Christian faith are its many beliefs about what exactly to expect. Most Christians believe that having a personal relationship with Jesus Christ, affirming his death and resurrection for the atonement of sins, and living and behaving with the knowledge of God's grace and eventual forgiveness, entitles one to enter into heaven. Judgment, in this case, has to do with God's question: "What did you believe about My Son?" In addition, there are thoughtful Christians who believe that the Bible could possibly infer that Christ's death was instrumental for everyone to enjoy eternal life. That belief is considered heresy by many. The question is whether Christ's work on the cross truly does open heaven for all people who seek and accept God's grace and love.

I would love to believe that. I would love to believe in a God who judges wisely and mercifully to all who want to experience His love. Pastor Rob Bell who, in 2011 wrote the book *Love Wins*, would like to believe the same thing. As much as I would love to believe this, I still have to wrestle with passages in the New Testament that challenge that belief.

The Life Review

Chapter Three of *After* is titled "The Life Review." Greyson reports that of the participants in his research, 25% reported a life review. Some of them told him that their entire lives flashed before their eyes, and others said that they were able to select and view different scenes from their lives at will. The life review was often described as more vivid than ordinary memories, as if on a movie screen or as pages in a book. Many experiencers stated that they felt these past events as if they were still happening with all the original sensations and feelings.

The very interesting thing about a life review is that they were experienced not only from their own vantage point, but also from the vantage points of those who were affected, especially the ones who had been harmed. From studying Greyson's report on life reviews, it seems that the purpose of the life review was not to inflict judgment or punishment as much as to receive redemption. Charles Dickens gave Ebenezer Scrooge a life review in his book *A Christmas Carol*. Recall that Scrooge was visited by four ghosts. The ghost of Christmas past chided a resistant Ebenezer that the purpose of the visitations was for his redemption and welfare. If people possess an actually working soul, they can see and feel the hurts and injustices they have inflicted on others. If they hadn't felt in life the full emotional impact of their actions because of that too-human tendency for self-justification and denial, they will in their life review. They will experience justice – not the harsh judgment that they may expect, but a sobering and redemptive review of their life on earth. Interesting to think about, isn't it?

Life Review Therapy

As a therapist, I've listened to a lot of people review their lives. Some of the stories are fairly benign, and some are horrific. So many times I've heard someone say, "I haven't told anyone this before." Over the years, I've observed that healing requires talking about painful things, often through tears, and accessing painful memories so that the brain can do its healing work of neural integration, lessening the intensity of the traumatic emotions.

Frequently, healing requires forgiveness – forgiving yourself and others. People who attend Alcoholics Anonymous meetings know how that works. Step number four requires undertaking a fearless and searching self-inventory and the following steps require seeking forgiveness and making amends to those whom you have injured. If you haven't done that yet, find a close friend that you trust or see your pastor, priest, rabbi, or imam, or contact a therapist. Systematic confession in many liturgical Christian churches is encouraged prior to taking communion. This is a great idea, reinforcing the notion that communion requires community. Full participation in community requires awareness and accountability for one's behavior. So, steel yourself with the courage fearlessly to face yourself, make amends, and when possible, be open to being forgiven as well as forgiving others. So many of the burdens that we carry in life are our soul's recognition that we have harmed ourselves by the harm we have done to others. It seems that Charles Dickens understood this: he wrote that when Scrooge woke up on Christmas morning following his haunting life review, he felt "as light as a feather." You can if you wish, wait to have your life review at the end of your journey. On the other hand, why wait until then?

More About NDEs

Many people who had a NDE report a sense of profound peace and calm. In some cases, people experience a sense of divine love. It isn't uncommon during a NDE for an experiencer to see themselves hovering over their body, looking down at their dying or dead self, and viewing themselves with acceptance and compassion and the urge to continue forward to their final home.

A striking commonality among NDE reports is the intensity of the otherworldly experience – penetrating light, a celestial glow, glorious colors, meadows of flowers glowing with colors dulled by the filtering brain. Experiencers have met other people in NDEs, some they recognize from when they were alive and others they had never met. Eben

Alexander, in his NDE, reports meeting a sister he never knew he had. These similar experiences have occurred for many people, each with their own individual descriptions.

I have a pet theory about the common experience of swift movement through a tunnel that people have reported following a NDE. I haven't checked this out personally as yet. My theory is that the tunnel people report is the blur of rapid progression from being in time to arriving at eternity. At one-point physicists were saying that nothing travels faster than light and at the speed of light, time stops. Apparently that idea has been qualified lately, but for the purpose of my pet theory, I can imagine that I will be slowing down as I arrive in that timeless realm where God is light. Just a thought.

I expect comments from other Christians who recall the apostle Paul's words in his second letter to the church at Corinth. He said that he would prefer being absent from the body and present with the Lord. But in this letter Paul isn't talking about the *mechanics* of transportation or transformation, Paul is simply saying that he's ready to finish his journey. Scripture doesn't describe in any great detail how we get to eternity and what to expect there. Whatever it is, it will be interesting – if not spectacular – those who have had near-death experiences teach us that.

CHAPTER 16

●

MEMORIES

God gave us memory so that we might have roses in December.
~James M. Barrie

Recall from Chapter 1 that among the things you have with you on your final journey are your memories, lots and lots of memories. You may not remember what you had for breakfast but you'll certainly remember your first love. Research tells us that our "episodic" or short-term memory may decline as we age. Okay, what we had for breakfast isn't that interesting but, oh, that first love!

Emotion lifts experience into awareness. The more emotion is present in an event, the more likely it will be retained in memory. And, bummer, negative emotions are often retained more often than positive ones. This makes sense, since the brain is very interested in not revisiting painful locations, people, and experiences. For example, you may recall a hurtful comment from childhood, a put-down from middle school, and a scolding remark from a parent or teacher years afterward. When a client of mine was a young boy, he remembers a mean cutting remark from a neighbor whom the youngster was simply trying to be kind to. Many years later he can feel the emotions from that incident. Too many of those negative experiences can injure your self-perception and self-worth. Those aren't the kinds of memories we want to take with us on our journey. Later in this chapter, I'll point out a burial plan for those murderous memories.

Most of us have some photos of those memories. My first camera was a Kodak Land Camera encased in brown leather with a strap. You unlocked the front of the camera from which extended an accordion-style lens. Remember those? Later I got an Instamatic with a revolving flash bulb. I thought it was so cool when I got a camera that I could set the flash automatically. I mention photos because viewing them evokes memories. And try this out: look at a few of your old photos and let yourself feel the emotions attached to them. Notice which photos evoke which emotions – some are good and some you'd rather forget. My granddaughter recently saw a photo of a younger me. "Grandpa, you *were* so good-looking!" Grandkids can be mean.

Luckily you may have some great memories as well. Hopefully, you have lots of them, but even a few will do. These are memories chock full of happy emotions that you can withdraw with interest from your memory bank. You can also make some fresh memory deposits tomorrow if you like. We'll talk more about that later. For now, let's look at the various types and functions of memory.

Memory and Survival

Most people think of memory as an image. However, memory is much more than an image flashing across the screen of your mind. Memory is often emotion, sometimes a sensation – a fragrance for example, or listening to a song from the 60s – and memory can also trigger a behavior, especially in someone suffering from Post-Traumatic Stress Disorder.

Here is an example of how memory triggers emotions: you're walking through your local grocery store, the Thanksgiving holiday is just around the corner, and then suddenly, for no *apparent* reason, you're in the best mood. You weren't conscious of the aroma of the pumpkin-spice candle on the shelf nearby, but it worked its magic. Images of family around the table, laughter, and good food fill your mind. Or, conversely, you're walking through your local grocery store and suddenly you feel nauseous. You weren't conscious of the aroma of the pumpkin-spice candle on the shelf but now you're flooded with dread. Thanksgiving means people drinking too much, loud arguments, yelling, and blaring football on the television, and you wish you could just get the whole holiday season over with.

Memory will do that. It can be triggered by the physical sensations of fragrance or music or the chill of fall weather. Memory will evoke images, emotions, and other physical sensations, including the impulse to pick up the phone and cancel Thanksgiving! However, some memories can also be wonderful. I'm certainly glad that the perfume, Taboo, is out of fashion today. My high school girlfriend wore that fragrance; one sniff of that intoxicating perfume would bring back the overwhelming emotions of my first love.

Fragrance, music, the time of year, even the time of day can stir an emotional memory. If you're retired, you may be finally over feeling the dread of Sunday evenings, the weekend coming to a close with the horror of having to return to school or work the next day. Sunday mornings were usually pleasant, but I recall that as the day wore on, my brain began to prepare itself for the loss of the delicious freedom of the weekend and the plunge back into the dread of daily obligations. But those are my memories and your memories may certainly be different.

In addition to emotional memory, there is often a behavioral trigger with certain memories. I was talking with a client one afternoon when his cell phone began ringing. The ringtone was the old-fashioned "briing, briing" that I grew up with. I found myself beginning to get up out of my chair to "answer the phone" as I had done for years and years before. I laughed at myself and sat back down. It isn't so funny when a veteran falls to the ground, ducking for cover, because of a loud noise outside. Memory may trigger behavior and action as well as emotion, often quite spontaneously.

Perhaps the most important role of memory is for the purpose of survival. Once upon a time, it would have been important for us to remember where the lion lives, where the enemies live, where the cliff is located. It was important to recall which fruit is poisonous, that there are crocodiles in the river, and how to behave around people you don't know or even people you do know. Memory has helped us to survive by triggering the emotions of fear or anxiety, emotions that alert us to danger and the need to be cautious or avoidant. So, because memory is essential for survival, our brains seem to be more interested in remembering things that can hurt us. I could easily finish this chapter by recalling all of the counseling sessions I've had over the years dealing with people who were plagued with horrible recurring memories of trauma. An unpleasant fact of brain functioning is the brain's tendency to hold on to information that either has or can hurt us. The information may have been useful at one time, but now those memories remain as emotional scars.

Memory and Emotion

Memory can trigger emotion and emotion is energy. When you think of a pleasant memory you may be aware of the good feelings that lay inside of that memory. What are some of your pleasant memories? If you are a parent, do you recall rocking or holding your infant? I know that physics would disagree, but didn't it seem like the little one felt heavier when he or she finally fell asleep? I recall the image but more, I recall the feeling. When I was rocking my infant daughter, for instance, it seemed that I could also feel God's love. That may be the closest a human being can come to knowing the love of our heavenly Father.

Why do you dig out one of your old scrapbooks - is it to see an image or to feel a feeling? Of course, it's both. You can't really disconnect one from the other. But you probably wouldn't have the same experience with someone else's scrapbook. Why do you even save photos in a scrapbook or spend hours creating a specially designed memory book? Is it because your memories hold more than happy images and happy emotions? Perhaps your memories also hold meaning. What kind of meaning do your memories hold? We'll explore that in a bit. For now, let's finish our discussion of memory and emotion.

Emotion is energy for protection and connection. Positive emotions such as love, joy, happiness, or contentment connect us with the welcome experiences of people and times that we value. These emotions prompt us to revisit those people and times and to refuel and reenergize ourselves for the daily tasks of living. Just going back to that scrapbook of images can have a similar effect of experiencing the energy of connecting with happy times with family and friends again. Among many other reasons, we stay close to people we love in order to be nourished by the experience of positive emotions.

Other Emotions

Emotions, as I've said, are physiological-psychological sources of energy for *connection* and *protection*. Love and happiness connect us to people and joyful experiences so we wish to stay close to both. The protective emotions of anger, fear, and sadness have the opposite effect (but not always). Anger is the energy to fix what isn't working, to take action in the short term to deal with an immediate threat, and in the long term to fuel the work of creating change. It is good to be angry at evil and then to work, when possible, to use anger's energy to make a difference in the world. Fear, of course, warns us of danger and energizes us to be cautious and take preventive action. Sadness is the energy necessary to let go of an attachment – an attachment to someone, something, or of happy times of our life. We grieve the loss of a loved one, a friend who has moved away, happy times from the past or, perhaps we grieve the loss of the vitality of our youth. In any case, these emotions are all important sources of energy, to move forward, to create change, or to let go.

A difficult challenge with emotions is that they are like two-sided coins. The other side of the coin of anger, for example, is passion. When people paint anger, they usually use the color red, but red is also the color of Valentines and Chinese weddings. When someone is repressing feelings of, say, anger toward their spouse, it's hard to want to be close to them. Courage isn't the absence of fear but the energy to face the fear and move forward against it. Feeling the blues of sadness is required for grieving a loss and arriving at a place of acceptance and the cool blue hues of peace.

Carrying Memory

I opened this chapter by saying that among the things you carry with you on your final journey are your memories, and you carry them whether you want to or not. While you certainly want to hold on to and celebrate your positive memories – visiting your scrapbooks or your iPhone photos from time to time – what do you do with the negative memories? I promised I would give you some suggestions.

The first thing to do is to try to locate and let go of memories that no longer serve any purpose. Recall that I said that memories of trauma, danger, or threat are useful and protective. If you no longer need those memories, here are some ways to let them go. This may seem counter-intuitive but one way to let go of old memories is to talk about them. When you talk about hurtful memories (I know they're painful to talk about) but your brain goes to work and actually metabolizes the emotion contained in the memory through the process I have described above. The net result, whether you feel the pain and cry or yell or break dishes, you feel better. Don't say you "broke down," say "you broke through" – you broke through a defensive barrier that kept these old memories locked away. (If you plan to break dishes, buy some at your local thrift store and break them into a large box or container so there's less mess to clean up. That takes away some of the fun of breaking the dishes but it's safer and less messy.) Or you could just yell and beat up your pillow (be sure it's a pillow and not a person). The goal here is catharsis, the release of pent-up negative emotion.

I'll give you an illustration. I once had a client who complained of depression. She told a story of working for a small business run by a husband-and-wife team who were constantly arguing. It reminded her of how her parents used to argue before they got divorced. Added to her stress was a recent break-up with her boyfriend. As she was relating her story, she began to tear up. Then she began to sob – these seemed like ancient racking sobs. As she cried, she grabbed a nearby sofa pillow, held it tightly to her chest, and began rocking back and forth. You don't have to be a professional counselor to see that she was regressing into a child-like state of self-soothing the way she did when she was little. I didn't want to intrude on her need to deal with this old traumatic memory that was surfacing into awareness. After a few minutes, when her sobbing died down, I said to her, "This may seem like a strange question, but how old do you feel right now?" She looked puzzled for a moment and said that she felt like a five year old, but then she looked startled and said, "Oh, my God, that was just after my dad left and Mom worked at nights and I would sometimes be left alone. I would go to the front door and sit and cry and rock myself to sleep." So that buried memory, when it surfaced, brought with it the image of a little girl crying alone, the emotion of abandonment and fear, and the rocking, self-soothing behavior, all released from within the split-off memory. No wonder my client was depressed - that's a lot to carry around in your soul.

Look up the topic of healing from memories for more insight into how catharsis and reenactment of traumatic memory works. The difficult part is feeling that something isn't right inside but not being able to put your finger on what it is. I encourage you to find a therapist that you feel comfortable with to help you to resurface those memories. Buried memories can cause unwanted emotions and self-defeating behaviors. If you've ever wondered why certain topics of conversation or images on television can be so troubling, it may be because they trigger memories, memories that you'd rather not think about. I'll give you an illustration.

While writing this book, I've also been working on a kind of autobiography. I don't imagine that anyone would be interested in reading it. I'm doing it to remember my life, to recall people and experiences that have shaped who I am. I'm writing to remember. I think I'll learn some things in the process. If there are buried memories that need to surface into awareness, so much the better. I don't want to hold on to shoes and shirts I no longer wear, books I've already read, or memories that caused me pain. But I do want to reflect on the lessons that they've taught me.

Forgiveness

In this writing process, if I do recall a person or situation that still causes me pain or regret, I plan to ask God for forgiveness. I'll ask God to forgive the person who hurt me and to forgive me when I'm the person who hurt someone. I'll also ask Him to forgive my mistakes, missteps, and missed opportunities. I would like to imagine that they were all a part of the learning I needed to do but, no excuses. Or maybe I didn't *need* to learn some of those lessons – maybe I was just selfish and thoughtless and stupid. The hopeful thing about being granted free will may be the possibility of the redemption of stupidity. I hope so. I need lots of that.

Recall my telling you about the young woman who came to see me because she was depressed. When she had regressed into that child-like state of sobbing and rocking, it was because of an old emotional memory surfacing into awareness. We talked about what she had remembered and our conversation opened up more memories. It's interesting how memory is connected – open one and others rapidly follow. Much of psychotherapy is retrieving buried memories. Why? Because certain memories may carry the negative emotions that burdened us with times of heaviness, hopelessness, isolation, and anxiety. Keeping those emotions underground often means needing to detour around people, places, and conversations. Underground emotions are debilitating. They limit our ability to move freely in life – they may rob us of joy.

At some point, when I think my client may be ready, I'll suggest that it would be good to consider forgiving the people who have hurt her. I'll suggest that she forgive her parents for the stress they placed on her, and that she forgive her mother for leaving her, at five years old, alone, abandoned, in a darkened apartment. I'll reassure her that forgiveness won't immediately take away the hurt. It is simply a move in the direction of letting go. It is transferring judgment to God. The memories may linger but the pain will mostly dissolve over time.

Lessening the Pain of Hurtful Memories

I would invite you to do the same with your hurtful memories. When you think back over your life, when you find yourself tensing up when a memory surfaces, or when you avoid looking at a high school yearbook or photo album, ask yourself to think about why that may be. It may help to close your eyes and imagine the person or situation in order to bring the memory closer to the surface, intentionally allowing the hurtful or angry emotions to fully surface. As an act of your will, consciously forgive the people who hurt you. Take some deep breaths, imagining that you are breathing in God's spirit of forgiveness, and then breathe out, imagining that you are breathing out the pain. Another technique people have used is to collect these hurtful memories by writing them out and throwing them into a fireplace or finding some other ways to dispose of them. Clearly, the idea is to create a point of departure so that if a hurtful memory surfaces, you can confidently say, "I've dealt with that, it's in the past, I've thrown it away." That's the point – to have a point of departure so when a negative memory surfaces, it can be quickly replaced by another memory, that of having given that memory to God.

Another way to lessen the pain of negative memory is to consciously create new positive memories. Pull out those old memory books and recall some of the joyful and fun times you've had with your family and friends. Get back to church or to wherever you're able to reconnect with positive people, with people of faith. Find a way to give back and enrich yourself by meeting a need in your community.

I was once given an assignment in school to write a paragraph titled, "My life as a victim." This may be a pretty easy assignment for some people. I had to reflect for a time on when I have felt victimized, but eventually I came up with a few illustrations. Then the instructor told us to rewrite the paragraph again with the title, "My life as a survivor." It was an interesting assignment. The point of the exercise was to invite students to appreciate that so much of what feels victimizing could be reexamined and reframed. Memory works the same way. When someone works on letting go of hurtful memories and hangs on to the ones that bring joy, that person can, over time, rewrite their life story. It becomes a story about finding what is good and powerful and what is possible in life.

The Flavor of Memory

Good memories are food for the soul – bad memories, not so much – feed on the good ones. I remember the Rachel Carson National Wildlife Refuge in the fall, walking through the quiet woods, softly, among the red and yellow leaves and chilled air – an occasional duck rustling the still waters and birds singing in the marsh. Kathe and I sat on a bench breathing in the beauty of the place and creating mental photographs. Feeding on that astonishing memory nearly brings me to tears. It was as perfect as any memory could be, except the memory of my wife walking down the aisle on our wedding day or rocking my infant daughter to sleep.

I wonder if some people avoid remembering nearly all of their memories, especially those of difficult periods of time in life. I understand that. Memories can be very painful for many reasons. The brain makes unbidden associations so that one memory can lead to another, then another, bringing to mind memories that you would rather forget. Even feasting on wonderful memories can bring tears. Of course they can – these are memories of the past, and the past is gone. Or is it?

I feed on memories of the past because many of them are so incredibly nutritious. It's a cliché to say that the people we've loved aren't truly gone if we keep them present in memory. It may be a cliché but I think that the saying is more true than we might think. Memory, you recall, is not just to re-call an image, it's also the emotions, sensations, and behaviors that my brain has held onto and internalized. I am the me that these memories inhabit: my mother's cheerfulness, my father's pride, my teacher's smile, my first love's kiss. Close my eyes, breathe in, and they are all there.

Memory has many flavors; some memories are painful while others are rich with emotional nutrition. I like looking at my photo albums of the people and places I froze in time – people and places that I can take out of where I placed them and warm them up with happy and nostalgic remembering. And I am grateful for them, and so grateful to be granted a life of collecting cherished memories that I can take with me on the journey from aging and beyond.

CHAPTER 17

———— • ————

"FROM STRENGTH TO STRENGTH"

You have power over your mind - not outside events. Realize this, and you will find strength.

~Marcus Aurelius

I recently came across another book that I would like to recommend: *From Strength to Strength* by Arthur Brooks, published in 2022. I'm happy to recommend the book because it's an excellent overview of the challenges facing adults in the second half of life. I'm also happy to recommend it because Dr. Brooks comes to many of the same conclusions that I listed in previous chapters. He confirms that we must not continue to hold too tightly to the accomplishments of the past but rather to seek new forms of identity and well-being in later life. These new forms of identity and well-being are found in spiritual growth, alternative sources of creativity, and strengthening ties with family and friends. In this chapter, I will include some quotes and ideas from the book that I think are especially insightful and beneficial.

Dr. Brooks writes: "In 2007, a team of academic researchers at the University of California, Los Angeles, and Princeton University analyzed data on more than a thousand elderly people. Their findings, published in the Journal of Gerontology, showed that senior citizens who never or rarely felt useful were nearly three times as likely as those who frequently felt useful to develop a mild disability and more than three times as likely to have died during the course of the study." (This makes me wonder if part of my agenda in writing this book fits the old academic dictum of publish or perish.)

Clearly, the challenge of feeling useful in your later years is the difficult task of finding something that you truly enjoy doing, something that grabs your interest. This may be especially difficult for those whose former careers or accomplishments were especially significant. How do you successfully retire from a career that daily produced tremendous meaning (or tremendous adrenalin)? There's a ship's bell attached to the wall of a financial institution in Los Angeles. I knew the executive who rang the bell every time his company's value increased by a million dollars. He rang it often. And what happens when you've been teaching young students for 40 years, many of whom returned to your classroom as adults to thank you for being the one who encouraged and inspired them on their life's journey? How do you top meaningful work like that?

I heard about a mail carrier who, on his last day of work, was surprised by an amazing turnout of blocks of people who came out to thank him because he always had a cheerful disposition and a friendly word when he delivered the mail. He carried more than the mail – he carried the gift of joy. I had my six-week haircut recently. The woman who cuts my hair is very friendly and talkative. I asked her if she enjoyed her work. "I wouldn't want to do anything else," she said exuberantly. My guess is that she enjoys her work, likes talking to people, and finds meaning in helping people look their best. She will likely continue to work as long as she can and, hopefully, cultivate other interests along the way.

A friend of mine recently retired after 40 years as a professor at a prestigious university. Over coffee, we talked about her future. "I'm ready for a change," she said. She could have continued teaching if she had wanted to. We laughed at the idea that we could both continue teaching until the second time we showed up for class in our pajamas. The school may well overlook the first time, but at some point, someone would gently suggest that it may be time to retire.

A study in the *Chronicle of Higher Education* showed that the oldest college professors tended to have the best teaching evaluation within departments. They found this especially in the humanities, where professors got their lowest ratings early in their careers and improved through their sixties and seventies. My friend fits the profile. She was one of the school's favorite instructors. Her students loved her. She admitted that it was hard to walk away from that kind of success and influence, but she felt, increasingly, that she had finished this part of her journey. I admire her courage but mostly I marvel at her ability to know when it was time to move on. How did she know?

The Inner Journey

In *Modern Man in Search of a Soul* (1963), C.G. Jung described the arc of life. The first half of life according to Jung, is focused on the ego's development in relation to the outer world. You recall from Chapter 2 that "ego" is a word that's used to describe the energy and focus on managing sanity, security, and significance. In the second half of life, after we've met most of our ego needs, our attention begins to turn inward toward a better understanding of what Jung termed our "Self." This turning inward and discovering less interest in some of the things that used to feel more important is often a cause of depression. I describe this midlife change and transformation in more detail in Chapter 2. It isn't a stretch to imagine that you have been on two journeys simultaneously – an outer journey, interacting and managing your place in the outer world, as well as an inner journey of self-discovery. Jung is right that after midlife your focus shifts increasingly away from the outer journey to the inner journey. But it's also reasonable to imagine that you began getting to know your Self at an early age. James Hillman's argument in *The Soul's Code*, also discussed in Chapter 2, is aligned with this assertion.

I think my friend would also agree that she has been on two journeys simultaneously – an outer journey as a professional educator for forty years, and an inner journey of increasing self-awareness. As she grew older, this inner journey has become more and more compelling, so that letting go of her profession was not letting go of her "Self." In fact, my guess is that now that she is no longer bogged down with less fulfilling aspects of her job such as lesson plans, staff meetings, and grading papers, she may well have the cherished time she needs to explore new directions and opportunities for her journey ahead. I think that the intoxication of new ventures may well answer the question of how she was able to let go of such a meaningful and rewarding career.

The inner journey is the journey to discover more of yourself – your Self, the part of you that knows better than you do who you are and what journey is calling you next. In religious language, this is your spiritual self. Jung wrote that the second half of life was a time of spiritual growth and discovery. If the outer journey pushes you to be responsible and productive, the inner journey pulls you toward transcendence. What is transcendence? It is getting outside of yourself enough to think about who you are when you're not defined by a role – when you aren't father, mother, son, daughter, worker, wealthy or poor. Those concepts are temporal. What does your Self want to do or be at this stage of your life? Transcendence is an invitation for discovery. Recall from Chapter 1 Eric Fromm's idea that transcendence was one of our five fundamental human needs. I placed transcendence on the vertical axis of my diagram, illustrating that the pull of transcendence is a safeguard against becoming bogged down in the comfortable familiar. Søren Kierkegaard, in his 1844 book *The Concept of Dread*, called this being "tranquilized in trivia."

The comfortable familiar is dangerous – there should be a surgeon general's warning. I can feel the gravitational pull of the sofa and television already beginning to weigh me down. I know where that will lead: to a lazy sluggish body and an apathetic mind. I think that's why Brooks recommends finding something to do that is truly fun or extremely interesting. I would add something that's rewarding or challenging. I wouldn't call going for a walk or going to the gym or taking a yoga class especially fun, but it can be very rewarding. Anything that pulls you away from the comfortable familiar may well keep you healthier. What about doing something that's challenging? According to

Daniel Amen in his 1996 book *Change Your Brain, Change Your Life*, staying active and learning something new may add years to your life. Keep your brain active and working. Enjoy a salsa dance class while you're learning French. Or maybe just go for a walk.

Winston Churchill was a busy guy. He was naturally depressed after being demoted from being the First Lord of the Admiralty in 1915, after the failure of the Gallipoli campaign, but he continued his busy schedule in public service. On a family holiday that same year, he picked up a paintbrush and began his inner journey as an artist. I saw an exhibit of Churchill's paintings from 1915 to 1951 at the Reagan Library in 1992. Some of it looked amateurish; others, breathtaking. I think that his inner journey kept him sane and kept his "black dog" at bay during bouts of depression over the years and the ups and downs of demanding work on his outer journey in public service.

It wouldn't be a stretch to consider that you are on two journeys as well. You are already familiar with the journey you have taken so far, dealing with the responsibilities of the outer world, keeping body and soul together and, perhaps, supporting a family as well. And you may have already awakened to an inner journey with interests and activities that have helped you to stay sane and resourceful. If you haven't yet discovered parts of yourself that have remained dormant, now's the time. I have a friend who, retired from the movie industry, is restoring vintage cars. I have another friend, a retired accountant, who stays healthy and socially active as an avid pickleball player. As I mentioned before, I had never heard of the sport until two years ago when someone said told me that you're not really retired unless you play pickleball. So I am and I do. My point here is that it doesn't particularly matter what this second journey is composed of as long as it's something you enjoy or is something that brings, fulfillment, purpose, or challenge to your life.

Any of those will do. You can be happy on your final journey because you have found a pastime that you enjoy, one that nourishes your soul. You can be happy on your final journey because you have found a sense of purpose and meaning for your life. Brooks writes, "I'm satisfied and living a life of purpose and meaning. I imagine myself say-ing to my wife, 'You know, I have to say that I am truly happy at this point in my life.' I think of the forces in this [my] future life that are most responsible for this happiness: my faith, my family, my friendships, the work I am doing that is inherently satisfying, meaningful, and that serves others." Brooks says that it may also be possible to find a second journey that is not only inherently enjoyable but also meaningful. And he adds three additional sources of well-being: his faith, his family, and his friendships. Throughout this book, you found me encouraging you that all of these resources are essential to have on this final journey of your life.

Some people quit their professions because they are burned out. They have been working out of balance for too many years. Those are the people to worry about. They're dead way before they died. My grandfather died at age 56. When he was thirteen years old, he signed on as a cabin boy on a steamer from Pescara Italy bound for Argentina. He worked at one job after another and sometimes two at a time. Like many Italian immigrants, he arrived in the U.S. with a couple of dollars in his pocket, stayed with a relative until he could find work, and when he found it, he never stopped working. I get it. Far too many people do not have the luxury of living a balanced life. For them, the notion of an inner journey of self-discovery must seem ridiculous. I wonder how many of our fellow citizens are in that category. We who have the luxury of living a balanced life should thank God every morning and every evening and live out of our gratitude each day.

More About Gratitude

What does that look like, to live out of your gratitude? I can think of several things. It certainly means valuing your life – not taking your blessings for granted. It must also mean evaluating your priorities and not wasting too much time on things of no value. I'm most certain that when someone feels blessed and grateful, they become a blessing to others. If they have money to give, they give it. If they have time to give, they give it. When they allow themselves to know their own value, they value others.

In a 2019 interview with Anderson Cooper, Stephen Colbert said, "It's a gift to exist, and with existence comes suffering. I don't want it to have happened [speaking of losing his father and brothers in a plane crash] but if you are grateful for your life... then you have to be grateful for all of it. You can't pick and choose what you're grateful for." *The Harvard Health Publication* of August 14, 2021, cited research to confirm what you already know, that a main source of happiness is daily practicing gratitude. You already know this because, if you're familiar with any of the faith traditions, you know that practicing gratitude is a common encouragement. You also know about the value of being grateful from the many internet encouragements you can't help stumbling across.

An April 3, 2015 article in *Psychology Today* lists "Seven Proven Benefits of Gratitude," ways in which cultivating the habit of being grateful is good for your health. There are paragraphs describing each of the seven ways in detail. I'll just list them:

1. Gratitude opens the door to more relationships
2. Gratitude improves physical health
3. Gratitude improves psychological health
4. Gratitude enhances empathy and reduces aggression
5. Grateful people sleep better
6. Gratitude improves self-esteem
7. Gratitude improves mental strength

Recall that in Chapter 6 I quoted the Irish poet, John O'Donohue who wrote, "When you walk on the earth with reverence, beauty will decide to trust you." The world can be ugly, brutal, and unfair. It takes no effort to see those things. When you practice being grateful and look for good things, you will see those as well. Walking on the earth with reverence means, among other things, seeing God's hand in the beauty that's around you. It is there if you look for it. What does

O'Donohue mean when he says that beauty will decide to trust you? That's a strange turn of phrase, isn't it? Maybe he means it exactly the way he wrote it, as if beauty could pick and choose whom to trust. Does he mean the spirit of beauty – is there such a thing? Or is he talking about our psychological state? Has our faith in goodness been so damaged that we have lost the ability to trust that anything can be good? Maybe beauty doesn't trust us because we don't trust that beauty can be real, that goodness is real, or that love is real. This is why he says that we need to walk with reverence.

Reverence is a decision, an attitude, to respect and honor the power of transcendence, your ability to get outside of yourself. That isn't easy. You need practice. Some people would recommend breathing exercises, meditation, relaxation, and stress management training. These are all great. I have another idea. Drive the California freeways. Drive the Italian autostrada, navigate a roundabout in Rome or Paris. These are excellent ways to perfect patience. If you can successfully transcend your emotions in these challenging ways, you can more easily access your spiritual strengths: patience, tolerance, gratitude, and a deepening of your life in prayer.

Connection and Happiness

Brooks describes the power of connection using an example from nature. What would you guess is the largest living organism on the planet? Give up? It turns out to be a grove of aspen trees. He writes about how "one stand of aspens in Utah called 'Pando' spans 106 acres and weighs 6 million kilograms. The amazing thing is that although each aspen looks like an individual tree, it isn't. It's part of a larger organism." The same is true of the magnificent giant sequoias. These huge redwood trees can grow to heights of 275 feet but have very shallow root systems, only about 5-6 feet deep. How can they manage to stay upright through high winds and storms over the centuries? The answer is that their roots are interconnected. The enlarged intertwined root system provides both nourishment and stability to the grove. So it is with human beings. John Dunn's poem, "No Man is an Island," illustrates the interconnectedness of the human race. Our roots go deep into our past and are spread wide across the earth. It may be truer today than ever before that human life is interconnected and interdependent.

In 2002, George Vaillant published *Aging Well: Surprising Guideposts to a Happier Life* based on research from a landmark Harvard study of adult development. Vaillant's successor, Robert Waldinger, said, "The clearest message that we get from this study is this: good relationships keep us happier and healthier. Period. The people who were the most satisfied in their relationships at age fifty were the healthiest at age eighty." Brooks confirmed this fact in his own research and goes on to say that "the relationships that best mitigate loneliness – the aspens closest to us that we need to cultivate – are romantic partnerships and close friendships."

Brooks further states that our cultural myth that falling in love and having romantic passion is the secret to happiness and life satisfaction is wrong. "The secret to happiness isn't falling in love; it's staying in love, which depends on what psychologists call 'companionate love' – love based less on passionate highs and lows and more on stable affection, mutual understanding, and commitment." Brooks quotes a researcher in the *Journal of Happiness*: "The well-being benefits of marriage are much greater for those who also regard their spouse as their best friend." This certainly applied to my father. I shared with you earlier that he told me, a few days before he died, that he had married his best friend.

What's the difference between a friend, and a "real" friend? Brooks lists some key points for cultivating your aspen grove of friendships:

- No matter how introverted you are, you cannot expect to thrive into old age without healthy intimate relationships
- For married people, a loving companionate spousal relationship is key to thriving
- Marriage and family are not adequate substitutes for close friendships, which should not be left up to chance

- Friendship is a skill that requires practice, time, and commitment
- Work friendships are not a substitute for real friendships, although they can also be satisfying if designed well

Brooks closes his chapter on friendship with a poem by Henry David Thoreau:

> Two sturdy oaks I mean, which side by side
> Withstand the winter's storm,
> And spite of wind and tide,
> Grow up the meadow's pride
> Above they barely touch, but undermined
> Down to their deepest source,
> Admiring you shall find
> Their roots are intertwined
> Inseparably

"An Exciting Adventure of Opportunities"

Brooks' final chapters explore the benefits of faith and growing spiritually. Many people, Brooks suggests, never give themselves the time or attention required to develop themselves spiritually, kicking the can of faith down the road of life. He encourages us to put our spiritual development at the forefront of our lives, which for him means scheduling time every day to tend to our spiritual nature. Brooks confirms that an important component to spiritual development should be your willingness to be vulnerable – to accept the fact that you are a fragile human being who will one day die. He encourages us to let go of our pride and embrace the grace of aging, doing what we can, and must, to live out our lives as meaningfully as possible.

Brené Brown wrote *Daring Greatly: How the Courage to be Vulnerable Transforms the Way We Live, Love, Parent, and Lead*. I agree with her, based on the title alone. It's interesting that the title of Brooks' final chapter is "Cast into the Falling Tide." It reminds me of the closing chapter of Becker's *Denial of Death*, when Becker said that the most any of us can think to do is to create something for ourselves and drop it into the confusion, making, as it were, a sacrifice to the life force. This isn't an exact quote but it's close.

Brooks begins his final chapter with an anecdote about fishing. He was given a bit of wisdom from an experienced fisherman that to catch a fish in Puget Sound, it is important to wait for the tide to go out and cast into the falling tide. He writes, "In this last lesson, we will learn how to cast into the falling tide – to get started on your transition – with energy and confidence. Indeed, your biggest life transition doesn't have to be a crisis or a period of loss, but rather can be an exciting adventure of opportunities you never knew existed."

That may be optimistic, but I admire the spirit. Look forward now to an uplifting, purposeful adventure of endless opportunities on this, your final journey.

Modern Elder Academy

The Modern Elder Academy was established to help people in midlife and beyond to navigate the challenges of that life stage. Brooks quotes Chip Conley, the originator of the Modern Elder Academy. "By the time the participants complete the course of instruction they must be able to respond to the following questions:

- What activities will you keep?
- What activities will you evolve and do differently?
- What activities will you let go of?
- What will you commit to doing in the next week to evolve into the new you?
- What will you commit to doing in the next month?
- What will you commit to doing within six months?
- In a year, what will be the first fruits to appear as a result of your commitments?
- What new activities will you learn?"

As I said, I like this book for two reasons – it is an excellent overview of the challenges facing older adults on their final journey, and I also like it because Brooks restates many of the same suggestions I made in earlier chapters. I like his final advice to us. It's a good reminder of how to keep our priorities straight. Instead of loving and worshiping things and using people, he advises: "Use things. Love people. Worship the divine."

BENEDICTION

As a Presbyterian Clergyman for eight years, I often closed a service of worship with the following benediction: "The grace of the Lord Jesus Christ and the love of God and the fellowship of the Holy Spirit be with you all - and all of God's people said: Amen."

I never felt the impulse to remind the congregation that the benediction is not simply a prayer, rather, it is a "bene diction" (good word), a blessing. In this, you needn't bow your head, but look directly at the person pronouncing the blessing. In this blessing, I would often raise my hand as if to touch each congregant on the head. In fact, when I pronounced a benediction at a wedding, I would lightly touch the head of the bride and groom, saying, "May the Lord bless you and keep you...." I touched each head and asked God to bless their way forward because, dear God, they needed that help.

Now I am reaching out in the pages of this book hoping to touch each of you with a divine blessing as you move forward on your journey. In one sense you are alone in your sailboat navigating the darks and lights of life. But in a larger sense, all of us who are old and also on our own final journey sail with you. I pray that you will be able to sense the care and community of the countless elders who are traveling alongside you on this journey from aging and beyond.

ACKNOWLEDGMENTS

———————————◆ ● ◆———————————

I want to acknowledge three people who have inspired my writing and improved it:

Carolyn Whitman, a former English language instructor, who read every page and made many valuable suggestions.

Jennifer Leigh Selig, my publisher, who encouraged the project and helped to fix my frequent redundancies.

Dennis Patrick Slattery, my dissertation advisor, long-time friend and mentor who continues to inspire and encourage me on my journey.

75588485R00125